HOME-KITCHEN FOOD STORAGE

Pantry-shelf Storage, Room Temperature

food item	storage time	keep in mind
baking powder, baking soda	18 months	keep dry, tightly covered
bouillon cubes & powders	1 year	
breads & rolls	3 days	in original wrapping
cake mixes	1 year	keep dry
cakes, baked	2-3 days	refrigerate if with cream or custard filling
canned foods, all kinds	1 year or more	use oldest first
coffee, vacuum can	1 year, unopened	store in refrigerator or freezer 1 week after opening
coffee, instant	6 months, unopened	store in refrigerator or freezer 1 week after opening
coffee lightener, nondairy	6 months	keep dry
cookies, packaged	4 months, unopened	1 week after opening
crackers	3 months	keep dry, tightly closed
crumbs, cracker/bread	6 months	keep dry, tightly closed
flour, all-purpose/cake	6 months	keep dry, tightly closed
frostings, mixes & canned	6 months	
fruit, dried	6-8 months	
gelatin, unflavored/fruit	6 months	keep dry
herbs & spices, whole	1 year	keep tightly closed
herbs & spices, ground	6 months	keep tightly closed
honey	1 year	do not refrigerate
hot-roll/quick-bread mixes	1 year	keep dry
jam, jelly	1 year	refrigerate after opening
molasses	1 year	
nonfat dry milk	6 months	keep dry; refrigerate after reconstituting
oil, salad & cooking	3 months	keep tightly closed
pancake, waffle mixes	6 months	keep dry, tightly closed
pasta	6 months, unopened	keep dry
peanut butter	6 months	2 months after opening
piecrust mixes	6 months	
pies & pastries	3 days	refrigerate cream, custard
pudding mixes	1 year	
rice, brown & wild	1 year	
rice, white	2 years	
rice, flavored mixes	6 months	
salad dressings	6 months	refrigerate after opening
sauce/soup/gravy mixes	3 months	
sauces/ketchup, barbecue	2 months	keep tightly closed
shortening, hydrogenated	8 months	keep tightly closed
soft drinks	3 months	
sugar, granulated	2 years	keep dry
sugar, brown & confectioners	4 years	
syrups	1 year	close tightly after use
tea, loose or bags	6 months	
tea, instant	1 year	
vegetables: onions, potatoes, rutabagas, sweet potatoes, winter squash	1 week	keep dry; provide for air circulation, will keep 2-3 months at 55°

Refrigerator Storage, Fruits & Vegetables
(in crisper or closed plastic bags)

food item	storage time	keep in mind
apples	1 month	or store at room temperature
apricots, avocados, pears, melons, bananas, grapes, nectarines, peaches, plums	5 days	ripen before refrigerating
berries & cherries	3 days	
citrus fruits	2 weeks	or store at room temperature
pineapples	2 days	
asparagus	3 days	
beets, carrots, parsnips, radishes, turnips	5 days	remove tops before storing
cabbage, cauliflower, celery, cucumbers, green beans, eggplant, peppers	1 week	
tomatoes	1 week	ripen tomatoes before refrigerating
corn on the cob	1 day	refrigerate in husks
lettuce, spinach, all green leafy vegetables	5 days	remove damaged leaves before refrigerating
lima beans, peas	5 days	leave in pods

Refrigerator Storage, Dairy Products
(tightly covered or wrapped)

food item	storage time	keep in mind
butter	2 weeks	
buttermilk	2 weeks	
cheese, spreads	2 weeks	if mold forms on hard cheese, remove before serving — it will do no harm
cheese, cottage & ricotta	5 days	
cheese, cream & neufchatel	2 weeks	
cheese, sliced	2 weeks	
cheese, in whole cuts	2 months	
cream, sweet/sour	1 week	ultrapasteurized, 1 month in original carton
eggs, whole in shell	1 month	
whites, separated	4 days	tightly covered
yolks, separated	4 days	cover with water
margarine	1 month	
milk, whole & skim	1 week	
milk, reconstituted nonfat, opened condensed & evaporated	1 week	

Refrigerator Storage, Meat, Fish & Poultry (uncooked)

food item	storage time	keep in mind
beef, pork, lamb & veal: steaks, chops, roasts	5 days	leave in store plastic wrap or rewrap loosely
ground & stew meats	2 days	
fresh sausage	2 days	
variety meats	2 days	
bacon, frankfurters	1 week	after opening
ham, canned	6 months	unopened
ham, slices	3 days	
ham, whole	1 week	
luncheon meats, cold cuts	5 days	after opening
sausage, dry & semidry	3 weeks	
fish, shellfish (all kinds)	1 day	keep closely wrapped
poultry, fresh or thawed	2 days	

Refrigerator Storage, Leftovers & Packaged Foods (after opening)

food item	storage time	keep in mind
broth, gravy, soup	2 days	tightly covered
cakes, pies: cream or custard fillings	2-3 days	
casserole dishes, stews	3 days	
coffee	1 week	after opening
coffee lighteners, frozen	3 weeks	after thawing
flour: rye, whole wheat, wheat germ	1 year	tightly covered container — not original package
fruits	3 days	
juices, beverages	6 days	
meat, fish, poultry	2 days	remove stuffing from poultry
nutmeats	6 months	tightly covered
pickles, olives	1 month	original container
refrigerated doughs: rolls, biscuits, cookies, breads	check final-use date on package; do not open until ready to use	
salad dressings	3 months	original container
salads: potato, chicken, fish, coleslaw	2 days	tightly covered
wine, white table	3 days	after opening

Continued on back Endsheet

Freezer Storage, Commercial Frozen Foods

food item	storage time	keep in mind
breads, rolls (baked)	3 months	overwrap commercial wrappings
breads, unbaked loaves	3 months	overwrap commercial wrappings
cakes: butter, pound-type	6 months	unfrosted, overwrap
cake, angel food	2 months	overwrap
cake, frosted layer	4 months	
coffee lighteners	1 year	
doughnuts, danish pastry	3 months	overwrap
fish (fat types): trout, mackerel, salmon	3 months	overwrap if package damaged
fish, (lean types): cod, flounder, sole	6 months	if thawed, do not refreeze
shellfish, breaded, cooked	3 months	
lobster, scallops	3 months	
king / queen crab	10 months	
shrimp, uncooked, unbreaded	1 year	
fruit	1 year	
ice cream, sherbet	1 month	overwrap leftovers
main-dish pies, fish or meat	3 months	
main-dish pies, poultry	6 months	
meats, beef roasts, steaks	1 year	overwrap
ground beef	4 months	overwrap
lamb, veal roasts, & steaks	9 months	overwrap
pork chops	4 months	overwrap
pork roasts	8 months	overwrap
pancake / waffle batter	3 months	
pies, unbaked	8 months	
pies, ready to thaw & eat	4 months	
poultry: chicken, turkey parts	6 months	
whole chicken, turkey	1 year	
duck, goose	6 months	
turkey rolls, roasts	6 months	
vegetables, all	8 months	

USEFUL SUBSTITUTIONS

if the recipe calls for	use instead
2 tablespoons all-purpose or whole wheat flour (for thickening)	1 tablespoon cornstarch or arrow-root or potato starch or quick-cooking tapioca
1 cup beef or chicken broth	1 bouillon cube or 1 envelope or 1 rounded teaspoon bouillon powder + 1 cup boiling water
2 egg yolks	1 whole egg
1 cup grated coconut	1⅓ cups flaked coconut
1 pound fresh mushrooms	12 ounces canned mushrooms, drained, or 3 ounces dried mush-rooms, rehydrated
1 teaspoon lemon juice	½ teaspoon distilled white vinegar
1 teaspoon grated lemon peel	½ teaspoon lemon extract
1 cup homogenized milk	1 cup skim milk + 2 tablespoons butter or margarine; or ½ cup evaporated milk + ½ cup water, or ¼ cup powdered whole milk + 1 cup water
1 square (1 ounce) unsweetened chocolate	3 tablespoons cocoa + 1 table-spoon butter or margarine
½ cup butter or margarine	7 tablespoons vegetable shortening
1 cup sifted cake flour	⅞ cup sifted all-purpose flour
1 teaspoon baking powder	½ teaspoon cream of tartar + ¼ teaspoon baking soda
1 cup sour cream (for use in cooking)	1 tablespoon lemon juice + evapo-rated milk (undiluted) to make 1 cup, or ⅓ cup butter + ¾ cup yogurt or buttermilk

1 cup buttermilk or sour milk	1 tablespoon lemon juice or white vinegar + milk to make 1 cup (let stand 5 minutes)
1 cup honey or corn syrup	1¼ cups sugar + ¼ cup liquid
1 tablespoon snipped fresh herb	1 teaspoon dried herb, same kind
1 medium onion, chopped	1 tablespoon instant minced onion, rehydrated
1 cup light cream or half-and-half	3 tablespoons butter + ⅞ cup milk
1 cup heavy (whipping) cream	⅓ cup butter + ¾ cup milk
2 cups tomato sauce	¾ cup tomato paste + 1 cup water
1 cup tomato juice	½ cup tomato sauce + ½ cup water
1 small clove garlic	⅛ teaspoon garlic powder or ¼ tea-spoon commercial garlic juice
1 tablespoon gelatin	1 envelope
1 cake compressed yeast	1 envelope active dry yeast
1 cup yogurt (in cooking)	1 cup buttermilk

FOOD-MEASURE EQUIVALENTS

start out with	to end up with
apples, 3 medium (1 pound)	3 cups sliced
bananas, 3 medium (1 pound)	1½ cups mashed
bread, 1-pound loaf	14 to 20 slices
bread, 1 slice (including crust)	½ cup crumbs
butter or margarine, ¼ pound	½ cup (1 stick or cube)
cheese, ¼ pound	1 cup shredded
cheese, cottage, 8-ounce container	1 cup
cheese, cream, 3-ounce package	6 tablespoons
chocolate, unsweetened, 1 square	1 ounce
chocolate, semisweet pieces, 6 ounces	1 cup
coconut, flaked, 3½-ounce can	1⅓ cups
coconut, shredded, 4-ounce can	1⅓ cups
cream, heavy or whipping, 1 cup	2 cups whipped
cream, sour, 8-ounce container	1 cup
egg whites, large, 8 to 10	1 cup
egg yolks, large, 12 to 14	1 cup
flour, all-purpose, 1 pound	about 3½ cups
flour, cake, 1 pound	about 4 cups
lemon, 1 medium	3 tablespoons juice, 1 tablespoon grated peel
lime, 1 medium	2 tablespoons juice, 1 teaspoon grated peel
milk, evaporated, 5⅓ or 6-ounce can	⅔ cup
12- or 14½-ounce can	1⅔ cups
sweetened condensed, 14-ounce can	1¼ cups
nuts, 1 pound almonds in shell	1 to 1¼ cups nutmeats
almonds, 1 pound shelled	3 cups
brazil nuts, in shell, 1 pound	1½ cups nutmeats
brazil nuts, shelled, 1 pound	3¼ cups
filberts, in shell, 1 pound	1½ cups nutmeats
filberts, shelled, 1 pound	3½ cups
peanuts, in shell, 1 pound	2 to 2½ cups nutmeats
peanuts, shelled, 1 pound	3 cups
pecans, in shell, 1 pound	2¼ cups nutmeats
pecans, shelled, 1 pound	4 cups
walnuts, in shell, 1 pound	2 cups nutmeats
walnuts, shelled, 1 pound	4 cups
onion, 1 large	¾ to 1 cup chopped
orange, 1 medium	¼ to ⅓ cup juice, 2 tablespoons grated peel
potatoes, 1 pound sweet, white	2¼ cups diced
raisins, 1 pound	3 cups
rice, long grain regular, 1 cup	3 cups cooked
salad oil, 16 ounces	2 cups
sugar, 1 pound granulated	2¼ to 2½ cups
brown, 1 pound	2¼ cups (packed)
confectioners, 1 pound	4 to 4½ cups
syrup, corn, 16 ounces	2 cups
maple, 12 ounces	1½ cups

Famous Brands

SOUPS & SALADS

Brand Name Publishing Corp.

Salade Niçoise (page 117); Chicken Pasta Salad (page 96); Marinated Tomato Salad (page 67); Fresh Fruit Salad with Poppy Seed Dressing (page 56). Mazola Corn Oil

Acknowledgments

The editors wish to thank the following companies for permission to use their recipes, photographs, and product names in this volume:

Almond Board of California

American Dairy Association

Armour Food Company/A ConAgra Company

Beatrice/Hunt-Wesson Foods

The William G. Bell Company

The Birkett Mills

ReaLemon® Lemon Juice from Concentrate Division of Borden Inc.

Wyler's® Bouillon Division of Borden Inc.

Calavo Growers of California

California Dried Bean Advisory Board

California Dried Fig Advisory Board

Campbell Soup Company

Carnation Company

Castle and Cooke Foods

Chicago Dietetic Supply, Inc.

Colombo, Inc.

CPC International Inc.

Cumberland Packing Corporation. Butter Buds®, Nu-Salt®, and Sweet 'N Low® are registered trademarks of the Cumberland Packing Corporation.

Del Monte Corporation

The Dow Chemical Company makers of SARAN WRAP™ brand plastic Film

Doxsee Food Corp.

Florida Department of Citrus

General Foods Corporation

General Mills, Inc. Bac-O's® is a registered trademark of General Mills, Inc.

A. Giurlani & Brothers

Gold's Pure Foods Corporation

Gorton's of Gloucester, A Division of General Mills, Inc.

Hamilton Beach Scovill Inc.

Heinz, U.S.A.

Herb-Ox Sales, Inc.

Hernke Foods, Inc.

Heublein Inc.

Geo. A. Hormel & Co.

Idaho Potato Commission

Kikkoman International Inc.

La Choy Products Company

Lawry's Foods, Inc.

Lea & Perrins, Inc.

Libby, McNeill & Libby, Inc., The Great Pumpkin Cookbook, A Harvest of Libby's Favorite Recipes. Libby's® is a registered trademark of Libby, McNeill & Libby, Inc.

Thomas J. Lipton, Inc., Englewood Cliffs, NJ 07632

McIlhenny Company

Minnesota Beef Council

Nabisco Brands, Inc.

National Pork Producers Council

Ocean Spray Cranberries, Inc.

Oklahoma Peanut Commission

Pet, Inc.

Pompeian

Ragú Foods, Inc., Owner of registered trademarks Ragú and Pizza Quick

Riceland Foods

Riviana Foods Inc.

Roquefort Association

Joseph E. Seagram & Sons, Inc.

Seneca-Kennett Foods

Sioux Honey Association

The J.M. Smucker Co.

Southland Frozen Foods, Inc.

Sunbeam Appliance Co., a member company of Allegheny International, Inc. Sunbeam® is a registered trademark of the Sunbeam Corporation

Sunkist Growers, Inc. Sunkist® is a registered trademark of Sunkist Growers, Inc.

Sun-Maid Growers of California

The Sweet Potato Council of the United States

Tennessee Pride Country Sausage

Uncle Ben's, Inc.

United Fresh Fruit & Vegetable Association

Ventre Packing Company

Vienna Sausage Manufacturing Company

Virginia State Apple Commission

Wisconsin Potato Growers Auxiliary

E. H. Wright Company

Wyler's® Bouillon Division of Borden Inc.

Invitation

The Famous Brands Cookbook Library invites you, the modern cook, to a new experience in your own kitchen. Have you ever wished you had a larger repertoire of company's-coming menus? Ever searched for a different and exciting way to prepare favorite products? Ever felt that if you could just have a certain technique explained simply, you could master an entire new world of cooking?

The solutions to these dilemmas and others are the cornerstone of the twelve volumes that comprise *The Famous Brands Cookbook Library*. Whether you are just getting to know your kitchen—or have a long-standing relationship with it—the recipes and hints provided here offer the very best and latest information available from the test kitchens of many of America's finest food companies. Once you have had a chance to discover the treasures inside this volume, you'll want to collect each of the other volumes in this series—and an invaluable home cooking library will be yours.

Famous Brands Desserts
Famous Brands Every Oven Microwave Cookbook
Famous Brands Great Vegetable Dishes
Famous Brands Meat Cookbook
Famous Brands Chicken & Poultry
Famous Brands Breads, Quick Breads, & Coffee Cakes
Famous Brands Soups & Salads
Famous Brands Pasta Dishes
Famous Brands Fish & Seafood Cookbook
Famous Brands Cooking with Eggs & Cheese
Famous Brands Main Dishes
Famous Brands Chocolate Classics

Published by Brand Name Publishing Corp., 1950 Craig Road, St. Louis, Missouri 63146 and Brand Name Books, Inc., 122 East 25th Street, New York, New York 10010.

Printed in Italy by Mondadori, Verona

Front cover: *Yogurt-Potato Soup (page 17)*. Idaho Potato Commission. *Dilly of a Deli Salad (page 105)*. Photo courtesy of Thomas J. Lipton, Inc. Back cover: *San Francisco Minestrone (page 31)*. Gordon E. Smith

Soups and Salads: Mealtime Magic

For a cookbook, what more natural a partnership, a good marriage, than soups and salads? When we want something uncomplicated, something light and simple, what else springs to mind but those friendly companions: a bowl of soup—brimming with down-home goodness—and a crisp and complementary salad.

Taken alone, each section is chock-full of every sort of classic recipe that you've come to expect from a fine basic cookbook. But at the same time, the cook who seeks a more exotic safari will be delighted to discover a wealth of exciting and unusual recipes, many featuring the unexpected ingredient that turns a meal into an adventure. For example: there's an entire chapter devoted to fruit and nut soups, many of which are delectable—as desserts! Thus, when you feel the urge to offer something unanticipated, surprise family or guests with one of these.

And in this one volume there's not just a garden of salads, there's a universe: shimmery molds; jewel-bright, refreshing fruit salads; a variety of greens and vegetables, tossed or marinated or arranged artistically; and, for the main event, hearty salads of pasta and rice and a myriad of meats. Plus a treasury of dressings, ensuring salad success for any occasion.

You'll find a plethora of useful hints and tips throughout the book—discussions about all kinds of salad greens; notes on preparing basic soup stocks; virtual glossaries of oils and vinegars; and ideas and instructions on how to garnish and glorify your creations.

In short, here is what every cook wants—kitchen-tested recipes; helpful information about techniques and ingredients; crowd-pleasing results—these are the pleasures of *Famous Brands Soups & Salads*.

Contents

Light Beginnings, Luncheon Favorites

To launch a meal or to be the heart of a light one—these soups do double duty as start-offs or go-withs.

Scotch Broth

Makes about 3 quarts

- 1½ **pounds lamb or beef cubes for stew, cut into 1-inch pieces**
- 1½ **cups chopped onion**
- 8 **cups water**
- ½ **cup regular barley**
- 8 **teaspoons Wyler's® Beef-Flavor Instant Bouillon or 8 Beef-Flavor Bouillon Cubes**
- ¼ to ½ **teaspoon pepper**
- 1 **bay leaf**
- 1 **cup sliced carrots**
- 1 **cup sliced celery**
- 1 **cup diced rutabaga or turnips**

Trim excess fat from meat. In Dutch oven, combine meat and water; bring to a boil. Let boil 10 minutes; skim off foam. Add onion, barley, bouillon, pepper, and bay leaf. Return to a boil; reduce heat and simmer covered 1 hour. Add remaining ingredients; cover and simmer 30 minutes longer, or until meat and vegetables are tender. Remove bay leaf before serving. Refrigerate leftovers.

Hot and Sour Soup

Makes 5 cups

- 1 **can (10½ ounces) condensed chicken broth**
- 2 **soup cans water**
- 1 **can (4 ounces) mushrooms, sliced or stems and pieces**
- 2 **tablespoons cornstarch**
- 2 **tablespoons Kikkoman Soy Sauce**
- 2 **tablespoons distilled white vinegar**
- ½ **teaspoon Tabasco pepper sauce**
- 1 **egg, beaten**
- 2 **green onions and tops, chopped**
  Chopped cilantro (optional)

Combine chicken broth, water, mushrooms, cornstarch, soy sauce, vinegar, and pepper sauce in medium-size saucepan. Cook over high heat, stirring constantly, until mixture boils and slightly thickens. Pour egg into soup, stirring constantly in 1 direction; remove from heat. Mix in green onions. Spoon into individual soup bowls; garnish with cilantro, as desired.

Consommé Shaw

Makes 8 servings

- 1 **large onion, minced**
- 1 **cup minced celery**
- 1 **carrot, minced**
- 1 **cup canned tomatoes, chopped**
- 3 **egg whites and the shells of 3 eggs**
- 2 **teaspoons white pepper**
  Pinch cayenne
- 3 **cans (10½ ounces each) Campbell's Condensed Beef Broth**
- 3 **soup cans water**
- 3 **bottles (8 ounces each) clam juice**

Combine all ingredients except clam juice and simmer covered for 1½ hours. Remove from heat and strain through several thicknesses of cheesecloth. Stir in clam juice and reheat. Garnish with finely chopped parsley.

Jellied Consommé with Sour Cream

Omit clam juice. Soak 2 tablespoons unflavored gelatin in ¼ cup water for 5 minutes. Stir into hot strained consommé until dissolved. Chill until firm. Beat with a fork and spoon into soup cups. Garnish each cup with sour cream.

Cream of Broccoli Soup (page 8); Cream of Mushroom Soup (page 8); Cream of Carrot Soup (page 8). Wyler's® Bouillon

7

Cream of Broccoli Soup

Makes about 1½ quarts

   4 cups chopped fresh broccoli, or 2 packages (10 ounces each) frozen chopped broccoli, thawed
   ½ cup chopped onion
   3 cups water
   2 tablespoons Wyler's® Chicken-Flavor Instant Bouillon or 6 Chicken-Flavor Bouillon Cubes
   ½ teaspoon thyme leaves
   ⅛ teaspoon garlic powder
   ¼ cup margarine or butter
   ¼ cup unsifted all-purpose flour
   ⅛ teaspoon pepper
   2 cups light cream or milk

In large saucepan, combine broccoli, onion, water, bouillon, thyme, and garlic powder. Bring to a boil; reduce heat and simmer covered 15 minutes, or until broccoli is tender. In blender or food processor container, using ⅓ broccoli mixture at a time, blend until smooth. Return to saucepan. Set aside. In medium saucepan, melt margarine; stir in flour and pepper until smooth. Stir in cream; cook and stir until thickened. Add to broccoli mixture. Heat through; do not boil. Refrigerate leftovers.

Cream of Mushroom Soup

Omit broccoli, thyme, and garlic powder; use 1 pound fresh sliced mushrooms and ¼ teaspoon ground nutmeg. Proceed as for Cream of Broccoli Soup.

Cream of Carrot Soup

Omit broccoli, thyme, and garlic powder; use 3 cups sliced carrots and ½ teaspoon basil leaves. Proceed as for Cream of Broccoli Soup.

Cream of Celery Soup

Makes 6 servings

   1 medium onion, quartered
   ⅓ cup butter or margarine
   6 to 8 ribs celery, cut into 1-inch pieces
   2 potatoes, peeled and cubed
   1 cup water
   ½ bay leaf
   ½ teaspoon salt
   ¼ teaspoon pepper
   2 cups milk, divided
   8 sprigs parsley
   ½ cup heavy cream

Blender-chop onion. Sauté in butter until golden brown. Put celery, potatoes, bay leaf, salt, and pepper into saucepan; cover and cook slowly 30 minutes, or until soft. Remove bay leaf. Put 1 cup milk into blender with half of cooked vegetable mixture and onions; cover and process at Purée until smooth. Pour into saucepan. Repeat with remaining mixture. When mixture is smooth, add parsley and process only until chopped. Add to mixture in saucepan and heat slowly. Add cream and seasoning before serving.

Homemade Bouillon and Consommé

Dear to the hearts of weight-loss dieters, bouillon—clear, largely defatted soup based on meat, fish, poultry, or vegetables—is a great deal more than a guilt-free supplement to a sparse meal. Usually a by-product of other cooking (the name comes from the French word for *boil*), bouillon was once, in the days of the back-to-the-stove stockpot, readily available to use as a plain soup, to be suitably added to or garnished, or to employ in cooking to enrich gravies, make sauces, and braise meats. Even though—in this country at least—the stockpot has vanished along with the cook who kept it going, bouillon can still be made at home, or it can be conveniently obtained by opening a can or by dissolving a cube of powder in boiling water.

Homemade bouillon is an excellent way of using up scraps and bones of meat or poultry not sufficient for a meal but too good to throw away. Long and slow cooking is the secret. Put bones and scraps, along with whatever flavoring vegetables you have on hand—onion, carrot, snips of parsley, celery—to cook in water, simmering for at least 3 hours. The water in which vegetables were cooked is a fine addition, and so are the leftover vegetables accumulated from several dinners. A bay leaf adds good flavor to beef, a pinch of thyme if the scraps are from poultry, rosemary or marjoram if lamb. Season to taste with salt and pepper a half hour before you plan on taking the bouillon off the stove. When done, fish out the bones and put the rest through a strainer, pressing with the back of a wooden spoon so that all the good essence of meat and vegetables goes through. Refrigerate, discard the fat that will rise to the top when the soup is chilled, and it is ready to use as you wish.

Isn't what you have made broth? Or consommé? Yes, it is. The 3 terms are used interchangeably now, although consommé is usually thought of as being more concentrated—more "cooked down"—than broth, and is clarified.

Cream of Mushroom Soup

Makes 4 servings

⅛ medium onion
1 cup sliced mushrooms
2 tablespoons butter or margarine
2 cups milk
2 tablespoons all-purpose flour
⅓ cup celery pieces
½ teaspoon salt
   Dash pepper

Place onion in blender; cover and process at Chop. Sauté onion and mushrooms in butter. Put remaining ingredients into blender; cover and process at Mix until smooth. Add mushrooms and onions. Process at Chop until mushrooms are finely chopped. Pour into saucepan and cook until thickened.

Curried Pea Soup

Makes 8 servings

2 tablespoons butter, softened
1 tablespoon all-purpose flour
2½ cups chicken broth
1 chicken bouillon cube
½ cup milk
1½ cups cooked peas
1½ teaspoons curry powder
   Salt to taste

Put butter, flour, and chicken broth into blender; cover and process at Beat until smooth. Empty into saucepan. Put remaining ingredients into blender; cover and process at Puree until smooth. Add to saucepan; mix well. Simmer until thick, stirring constantly.

Creamy Garden Soup

Makes 6 to 8 servings

2 cups chopped onion
¾ cup green onion slices
¼ cup butter or margarine
3 cans (10¾ ounces each) chicken broth
1 can (16 ounces) Libby's Solid Pack Pumpkin
¼ cup chopped parsley
1 bay leaf
½ teaspoon salt
½ teaspoon curry powder
¼ teaspoon ground nutmeg
⅛ teaspoon pepper
2 cups half and half

In large saucepan, sauté onion and green onion in butter. Stir in broth, pumpkin, parsley, bay leaf, curry powder, nutmeg, and pepper. Bring to boil. Reduce heat; simmer uncovered 15 minutes, stirring occasionally. Remove bay leaf. Transfer soup in 2-cup portions to blender container or food processor. Cover; blend at medium speed until smooth. Repeat with remaining soup. Return to saucepan; stir in half and half. Heat thoroughly. Serve chilled, if desired.

Quick Pumpkin Soup

Makes 6 servings

3 cups canned pumpkin
3 cups scalded milk
1 tablespoon butter
2 tablespoons Sue Bee Honey
   Dash ground nutmeg
   Dash ground cinnamon
   Pinch saffron
   Salt and pepper to taste
½ cup ham, cut into small julienne strips

Add pumpkin to scalded milk. Blend. Stir in butter, Sue Bee Honey, spices, salt, and pepper. Add ham and heat, but be careful not to boil.

French Onion Soup

Makes 6 to 8 servings

1½ pounds yellow onions
¼ cup butter or margarine
2 tablespoons salad oil
1 teaspoon salt
   Pinch sugar
2 tablespoons all-purpose flour
2 quarts canned beef bouillon
½ cup dry white wine
   Salt and pepper
   Toasted French bread slices
   Grated Swiss or Parmesan cheese

Peel and cut onions into very thin slices. Set dial of Sunbeam Multi-Cooker Frypan at 300°F. Melt butter with salad oil. Add onions and simmer about 10 minutes. Sprinkle salt and sugar over onions. Raise heat to 325°F. and cook until onions are tender and golden brown, stirring occasionally. Sprinkle flour over top of onions and stir 2 minutes. Stir in beef bouillon and wine. Taste and add salt and pepper, if necessary. Cover and simmer 30 to 40 minutes. Serve piping hot with slices of toasted French bread and Swiss or Parmesan cheese.

Potato Avocado Soup

Makes 4 servings

> 5 slices bacon, cut into small pieces
> 1 cup minced onion
> 2 medium potatoes, pared and cubed
> 3 cups chicken broth
> 2 Calavo avocados, peeled, seeded, and cubed (reserve ¼ of 1 avocado)
> ½ cup sour cream
>   Ground pepper
>   Salt

Fry bacon until crisp. Remove bacon and add minced onion to hot fat; sauté until tender, about 5 minutes. Add potatoes and chicken broth. Heat to boiling, reduce heat, and simmer until potatoes are tender, about 15 minutes. Remove from heat and add avocado. Purée mixture in blender or food processor. Return purée to pan and heat to boiling. Remove from heat and stir in sour cream. Salt and pepper to taste. Garnish with bacon and avocado.

Hearty Golden Soup (page 37); Creamy Garden Soup (page 9); Sopa de Calabaza (page 37). Libby, McNeill & Libby, Inc., The Great Pumpkin Cookbook, A Harvest of Libby's Favorite Recipes

Tangy Spinach Soup

Makes 4 servings

> 1 package (10 ounces) frozen chopped spinach, thawed
> 2 tablespoons butter or margarine
> 2½ cups milk
> 2 tablespoons all-purpose flour
>   Dash thyme
>   Dash ground nutmeg
> 1 cup diced Armour Star Salt Pork
> ¾ cup sour cream

Combine spinach and butter in saucepan; cook covered 5 minutes. Pour into blender; add 1 cup milk. Blend until smooth. Add remaining milk, flour, and seasonings; blend. Return mixture to saucepan; cook over medium heat, stirring occasionally, until thickened, about 10 minutes. Fry salt pork until crisp and light brown; drain. Stir ¾ cup salt pork and ½ cup sour cream into soup; pour into bowls. Garnish with remaining salt pork and sour cream.

Doctoring Canned Soups

Although they are very convenient, canned soups do not always taste the way you'd like them to. They can often be improved.

- Simmer 4 cups canned broth with ½ cup minced carrots, onion, and some celery and season with 3 or 4 sprigs parsley, ½ bay leaf, and a pinch of thyme.
- Enhance chicken broth with ½ cup dry white wine; add ½ cup red wine and several teaspoons tomato paste to beef broth; simmer about 30 minutes and strain before serving.
- Choose compatible kinds of canned soups and mix them togther for a taste variation—for example, tomato with onion; New England clam chowder with cream of poatato soup; cream of mushroom and golden mushroom.
- Brown ground meat and add to beef vegetable soup for more texture and taste. Add leftover cooked chicken, cut into bite-size pieces, to chicken noodle or vegetable soup. Stir leftover vegetables or canned vegetables into the soup while it is heating.
- Dilute condensed soups with milk or cream instead of water.
- Garnish soups with fresh ingredients of the particular soup; for example, mushroom slices on cream of mushroom; broccoli flowerets on cream of broccoli. Or try fresh sprigs of parsley on creamy tomato or lemon slices on clear consommé.

Doctoring Canned Soups (page 10)

Cream of Split Pea Soup

Makes 8 servings

    2 cups dried split peas
    2 quarts water
    1 onion, sliced
    2 stalks celery, sliced
    1 carrot, sliced
    1 ham bone
    ¼ bay leaf
    3 cups milk
    2 tablespoons butter or margarine
    1 teaspoon salt
    ⅛ teaspoon pepper
      Chopped parsley

Wash peas. Soak in cold water several hours or overnight. (If quick-cooking peas are used, do not soak.) Put peas, onion, celery, carrot, ham bone, and bay leaf in Sunbeam Multi-Cooker Frypan. Bring to boil at 300°F. Set dial at Simmer. Cover and simmer about 2 hours, or until peas are tender. Turn off heat and let cool slightly. Remove ham bone and bay leaf. Place part of mixture into blender. Cover and process at Purée until smooth. Continue to process remaining mixture. Return smooth mixture to Frypan. Add milk, butter, salt, and pepper. Heat at 300°F., but do not boil. Sprinkle with chopped parsley before serving.

Purée of Mongole Soup

Makes 8 to 10 servings

    1 pound (2 cups) yellow split peas
    1 medium onion, diced
    2 large carrots, diced
    1 cup sliced celery
    1 teaspoon white pepper
    ¼ teaspoon grated nutmeg
    1 can (10½ ounces) Campbell's Condensed
        Consommé
    1 can (10¾ ounces) Campbell's Condensed
        Tomato Soup
   10 cups water
    1 smoked ham hock
      Finely chopped parsley
      Crisp croutons

Combine all ingredients in a large kettle. Bring to a boil, lower heat, and simmer for 1 hour, or until split peas are very soft. Remove ham hock. Press soup through a sieve or food mill, or whirl in a blender. Serve garnished with finely chopped parsley and crisp croutons.

Classic Cream of Tomato Soup

Makes 8 servings

¼ **pound butter or margarine**
2 **tablespoons olive oil**
1 **large onion, thinly sliced**
½ **teaspoon dried thyme**
½ **teaspoon dried basil**
   Salt and pepper to taste
2½ **pounds fresh ripe tomatoes, quartered, or 1 can**
     (2 pounds 3 ounces) tomatoes, preferably
     Italian style
3 **tablespoons tomato paste**
¼ **cup all-purpose flour**
3¾ **cups fresh or canned chicken broth**
1 **teaspoon sugar**
1 **cup heavy cream**

Preheat Sunbeam Multi-Cooker Frypan to second M in Simmer. Add butter; when melted add olive oil. Add onion, thyme, basil, salt, and pepper. Cook, stirring occasionally, until onion is wilted. Add tomatoes and tomato paste; stir to blend. Cook 10 minutes. Place flour in small bowl; add about 5 tablespoons of the broth, stirring to blend. Stir into tomato mixture. Add remainder of broth; cook 20 minutes, stirring frequently. Process soup in quarters or thirds at Purée in blender. Return to Frypan and stir in sugar and cream. Heat until serving temperature.

Hot and Cold Ideas

Sometimes a little of whatever ingredient you have made the soup from is a just-right garnish. Try using 2 thin slices of scored, unpeeled cucumber on cold cucumber cream, a lengthwise slice of avocado on avocado cream. Shredded raw beets make a beautiful surprise addition to borscht. A carrot curl or carrot shreds dress cream of carrot; whole spinach leaves float gracefully on cream of spinach; and small, raw celery sticks stuffed into pitted ripe olives make a colorful bonus for cream of celery soup.

Sometimes contrast is called for. On a curried cream soup, hot or cold, float a thin slice of a cored, unpeeled apple—dunk the slice in lemon juice first so that it won't darken. Half a deviled egg is a fine idea for any seafood bisque, or sprinkle such soups with tiny shrimps and snipped chives or parsley or chopped celery leaves.

Popcorn (unbuttered) sits up perkily on the surface of soup and tastes good, too. Raw onion rings or green pepper rings make a pretty, tasty soup garnish. So do canned French-fried onions, Chinese noodles, slices of sausage, crumbled bacon, chopped or sliced olives, oyster or cheese crackers, halved pretzel sticks, or a handsome whole large pretzel.

Tomato Bisque à la Claudine

Makes 6 servings

2 **cans (11 ounces each) Campbell's Condensed**
    Tomato Bisque Soup
1 **cup heavy cream**
1 **cup sherry**
½ **teaspoon oregano**
   Salt and pepper
   Garlic powder

Combine all ingredients with salt, pepper, and garlic powder to taste. Simmer, stirring occasionally, until very hot, about 15 minutes. Serve topped with sour cream and croutons.

Cream of Vegetable Soup

Makes 4 to 6 servings

2 **cups milk**
½ **cup pared, cooked, and cubed potatoes**
1½ **cups cooked or canned vegetables**
1 **thin slice onion**
1 **teaspoon celery salt**
¼ **teaspoon dried dill weed (optional)**
⅛ **teaspoon pepper**
½ **cup light cream**
   Salt to taste
   Chopped parsley (optional)

Put all ingredients except salt and parsley into blender container in order listed. Cover; blend at low speed until smooth. Pour into saucepan; heat gently just until simmering. Add salt. Serve hot or chilled, garnished with chopped parsley, if desired.

Egg Drop Soup

Makes 1 quart

1 **tablespoon cornstarch**
4 **cups water**
4 **teaspoons Wyler's® Chicken-Flavor Instant**
    Bouillon or 4 Chicken-Flavor Bouillon Cubes
1 **egg, well beaten**
   Sliced green onion

In 1-cup measure, stir cornstarch into ½ cup water. In medium saucepan, combine remaining water, cornstarch mixture, and bouillon. Cook, stirring occasionally, until bouillon dissolves. Slowly pour in the egg; stir. Heat through. Garnish with onion.

Chinese Watercress Soup

Makes 4 to 6 servings
    1 bunch watercress
    ¼ pound lean pork, finely diced
    1 teaspoon cornstarch
    ½ teaspoon pepper
    ¼ teaspoon sugar
    ½ teaspoon grated fresh ginger root
    1 tablespoon soy sauce
    1 tablespoon peanut oil
    2 cans (10½ ounces each) Campbell's Condensed
        Chicken Broth
    2 cups water

Wash watercress and trim heavy stems. Chop watercress finely. Mix pork, cornstarch, pepper, sugar, ginger root, and soy sauce. Heat oil and brown pork mixture. Add chicken broth and water and bring to a boil; simmer 10 minutes. Add watercress and simmer another 5 minutes.

Senegalese Soup

Makes 4 to 6 servings
    ¼ cup chopped onion
    1 medium clove garlic, minced
    2 teaspoons curry powder
    1 tablespoon butter or margarine
    1 can (11¼ ounces) Campbell's Condensed Green
        Pea Soup
    1 can (10½ ounces) Campbell's Condensed
        Cream of Chicken Soup
    1½ soup cans milk
        Cucumber or apple slices

In a saucepan, cook onion with garlic and curry in butter until tender. Gradually blend in soups and milk until smooth. Cook 5 minutes, stirring occasionally. Stir before serving. Thin with additional milk, if desired. Garnish with cucumber or apple slices.

A Matter of Taste

Seasoning a soup is a matter of taste. It is best to season when the soup is nearly done, however, because soup cooks down as it simmers, thereby intensifying and concentrating the flavors that have been incorporated. This is particularly true of salt, which is present in varying amounts in any stock-based soup. Typically, your homemade stock will probably already be seasoned to suit your palate. But canned or dehydrated stocks are unpredictable. Therefore, add salt and pepper toward the end of cooking time, being careful not to be too timid. A bland soup is no one's favorite.

Low-Cal Vegetable Soup Oriental

Makes about 6 servings
    5 beef bouillon cubes
    5 cups boiling water
    2 teaspoons Lea & Perrins Worcestershire Sauce
    1 teaspoon soy sauce
    1 cup thinly sliced carrots
    ½ cup sliced scallions or green onions
    2½ cups (½ pound) sliced mushrooms
    ¼ pound torn spinach

In a medium saucepan, combine bouillon cubes, water, Lea & Perrins, and soy sauce. Bring to boiling point, stirring to dissolve bouillon cubes. Add carrots and scallions. Return to boiling point. Reduce heat and simmer covered for 10 minutes. Add mushrooms and spinach. Cover and simmer 5 minutes longer.

Sopa Castilla la Vieja

Makes 6 servings
    3 cans (10½ ounces each) Campbell's Condensed
        Consommé
    3 soup cans water
    ½ cup ground blanched almonds
    1 tablespoon olive oil
    3 slices bread, toasted and cut into 1-inch strips
    ⅓ cup grated Parmesan cheese
    ½ cup toasted sliced almonds

Heat consommé and water. Mix almonds and oil and add to soup. Beat until well blended. Spoon soup into individual heatproof bowls. Top bowls with toast strips. Sprinkle with cheese. Broil until cheese is golden. Sprinkle with sliced almonds.

Clear Japanese Soup

Makes about 8 servings
    1½ quarts chicken broth
    ⅓ cup dry sherry
    4½ teaspoons Kikkoman Soy Sauce
    1 lemon, thinly sliced
    5 to 6 mushrooms, thinly sliced
    2 green onions, sliced diagonally
    1 carrot, cut into very thin slices

Bring broth to a simmer in large saucepan. Add sherry and soy sauce; simmer 2 to 3 minutes. Ladle soup into small bowls or mugs; float a lemon slice in each bowl. Arrange and present mushrooms, green onion, and carrot slices on a tray and have guests add their own garnishes to soup.

Frosty Soups

A cupful of cool soup is always refreshing, perfect for al fresco affairs when temperatures soar.

Jewel Consommé

Makes 4 servings

  1 envelope Knox® Unflavored Gelatine
  3 envelopes instant beef or chicken flavor broth
  ½ cup cold water
1¾ cups boiling water
  2 tablespoons lemon juice
    Garnishes (suggestions follow)

In a medium bowl, mix Knox Unflavored Gelatine and broth powder with cold water; let stand 1 minute. Add boiling water and stir until gelatine and broth are completely dissolved. Stir in lemon juice. Chill until softly set, about 3 hours. To serve, spoon into cups; garnish as desired.

Garnishes: If you like, top each serving with one of the following: snipped parsley, chives, or watercress; a dollop of unsweetened whipped cream or sour cream; packaged croutons or broken pretzel sticks; sliced green onions; sieved hard-cooked egg; finely chopped green pepper, celery, or cucumber.

Superb Asparagus Soup

Makes 4 servings

1 package (10 ounces) frozen asparagus
1 cup chicken broth
2 raw mushrooms, quartered
1 tablespoon minced onion
½ teaspoon salt
¼ teaspoon chili powder
½ teaspoon lemon juice
1 cup light or heavy cream

Break up frozen asparagus and place in blender. Add broth, mushrooms, onion, seasonings, and lemon juice. Cover and process at Purée 1 minute. Add cream, process at Stir 30 seconds. Serve cold.

Gazpacho (page 19). Campbell Soup Company

Jellied Borscht

Makes twelve ½-cup servings

  5 large beets
  1 cup chopped fresh onion
1½ teaspoons salt
4½ cups cold water, divided
  2 teaspoons sugar
  2 teaspoons fresh lemon juice
  2 envelopes unflavored gelatin
1½ cups sour cream

Wash beets, pare, and chop to make approximately 6 cups chopped beets. Place beets, onion, and salt in large saucepan, add 4 cups water, and bring to a boil. Reduce heat, cover and simmer 35 minutes, until beets are tender. Strain, reserving both chopped vegetables and liquid. Add sugar and lemon juice to liquid and return to saucepan. Heat to boiling. Sprinkle gelatin over remaining ½ cup water to soften. Add to boiling beet liquid; stir until gelatin dissolves. Remove from heat. Chill, stirring occasionally, until slightly thickened. Reserve 1 cup cooked beets and fold remaining beets into chilled gelatin mixture. Turn into bowl and chill until gelled (mixture will be soft). To serve, spoon ½ cup mixture into chilled soup cup. Top with 2 tablespoons sour cream and sprinkle with reserved beets.

Blender Sour Cream Borscht

Makes 4 servings

2 cups sour cream, divided
½ small lemon, peeled and seeded
¼ teaspoon salt
¼ teaspoon celery salt
¼ teaspoon onion salt
1 cup diced cooked beets

Put 1¾ cups sour cream and all remaining ingredients into blender; cover and process at Purée until smooth. Serve icy cold, garnished with remaining sour cream.

Chilled Carrot-Basil Soup

Makes about 3½ cups

    2 cups sliced cooked carrots
 1½ cups light cream or half and half
    1 can (10¾ ounces) condensed cream of
       mushroom soup
    1 teaspoon dried basil
  ½ teaspoon sugar
    Dash pepper

Place carrots, ¾ cup of cream, condensed soup, basil, sugar, and pepper in blender container; cover. Blend until almost smooth. Add remaining half of cream. Blend until well combined. Chill covered 3 to 4 hours to allow flavors to blend.

Chilled Corn Soup

Makes 4 servings

    1 can (16 ounces) creamed yellow corn
  ½ cup chicken broth
    1 cup half and half
    1 tablespoon Sue Bee Honey
    1 teaspoon paprika
    Salt and pepper to taste

Purée all ingredients except paprika, salt, and pepper in a blender or food processor until mixed. Season with paprika, salt, and pepper to taste. Stir well. Refrigerate soup until ready to serve.

Cold Red Pepper Soup

Makes 6 cups

    2 cans (13¾ ounces each) (3½ cups) chicken
       broth
    2 cups chopped red pepper
 1½ cups sliced leek
  ½ cup Idaho® Instant Mashed Potato Granules
    2 cups buttermilk
    1 tablespoon chopped fresh dill or ½ teaspoon
       dried dill weed
    Salt
    Pepper

In a large saucepot, combine broth, pepper, and leek; cover; bring to boiling. Reduce heat; simmer 10 minutes, until vegetables are tender. Purée vegetables with cooking liquid in a food processor or blender. Pour into a bowl. Stir in instant potato granules. Cover. Refrigerate until very cold. Stir in buttermilk and dill. Season with salt and pepper. If a thinner soup is desired, add more broth, buttermilk, or water.

Chilled Pea Soup

Makes 5 to 6 servings

    1 envelope Knox® Unflavored Gelatine
  ½ cup cold water
    2 envelopes instant chicken-flavor broth
 1½ cups boiling water
    1 package (10 ounces) frozen peas
    1 tablespoon grated onion
  ½ teaspoon salt
  ¼ teaspoon white pepper
  ⅛ teaspoon ground cardamom (optional)
    1 cup light or heavy cream
    Croutons (optional)
    Mint leaves (optional)

In a 5-cup blender container, sprinkle Knox Unflavored Gelatine over cold water; let stand 3 to 4 minutes. Add broth powder and boiling water; cover and blend 1 minute at low speed. Add peas, onion, salt, pepper, and cardamom. Blend at medium speed 2 minutes, or until peas are puréed. Add cream; process 1 minute. Pour into a medium bowl; chill until set, about 3 hours. Spoon into cups to serve. If desired, garnish with croutons or mint leaves.

Note: This soup will not become firm, but will have a soft-gel set, the proper consistency for a gelled soup. In case you're wondering, no cooking is required, not even for the peas!

Consommé à la Madrilène

Makes 4 servings

    1 envelope unflavored gelatin
    2 Herb-Ox Chicken Bouillon Cubes or 2
       teaspoons Herb-Ox Instant Chicken Style
       Bouillon
    1 cup cold water
    2 cups tomato juice
    Dash hot pepper sauce
    Lemon wedges

Sprinkle gelatin on cold water to soften; let stand 5 minutes. Stir over low heat until gelatin dissolves; add bouillon, stir to dissolve. Add tomato juice and hot pepper sauce. Heat to serving temperature. Or chill until set, stir with a fork. Serve with lemon wedges.

Yogurt-Potato Soup

Makes 6 cups

    2 cups frozen Idaho® Hash Brown Potatoes
      Salted boiling water
    2 cups plain yogurt
    1 cup pared diced cucumber
    1 clove garlic, minced
    1 teaspoon salt
    ½ teaspoon celery seed
    1 cup water
    2 tablespoons olive oil
    ½ cup chopped walnuts

In a medium saucepan, combine potatoes with 1 inch boiling, salted water. Cover, reduce heat. Simmer 7 to 10 minutes, until potatoes are tender. Drain. In a large bowl, combine potatoes, yogurt, cucumber, garlic, salt, celery seed, and water; mix well. Gradually stir in oil. Cover. Refrigerate 1 hour, or until thoroughly chilled. Serve sprinkled with walnuts.

Vichyssoise

Makes 4 to 6 servings

    2 cups peeled cubed potatoes
    ¾ cup leek pieces
    2 cups chicken broth
    1 cup milk
    1 teaspoon salt
      Dash white pepper
    1 cup light cream
      Chopped chives

Blender-chop potatoes and leek. Pour into a saucepan and cook until potatoes are tender. Put remaining ingredients except cream and chives into blender. Add cooked mixture; cover and process at Purée until smooth. Pour into bowl and stir in cream. Chill thoroughly before serving. Garnish with chopped chives.

Marvelous Madrilene

Consommé madrilène is a delicately flavored clear soup whose flavor is owed equally to meat stock and tomatoes; it is a handsome dark red. Served hot or cold—when cold, it is virtually always jellied—madrilène makes a delicious, not-too-filling first course.

Madrilène is available canned; shake the can well and store in the refrigerator to gel in about 24 hours. Or open the can, add to the madrilène 1 tablespoon lemon juice, a dash of hot pepper sauce, and 1½ cups finely diced vegetables—celery, green onions, green pepper, cucumber—in proportions to taste. Spoon into the cups in which it will be served; refrigerate covered 24 hours. Rather like an easy-do, soft-gel gazpacho.

Creamy Goddess Soup

Makes 4 servings

    2 cans (10½ ounces each) cream of potato soup
    1 tablespoon deviled ham
    ½ cup sour cream
    1 cup milk
    ½ teaspoon Worcestershire sauce
      Dash pepper
    ¼ cup snipped chives

Combine all ingredients except chives in a mixing bowl. Mix well. Chill. Serve cold, topped with chives.

No-Cook Cucumber Soup

Makes 6 servings

    4 cups buttermilk
    1½ cups finely diced cucumber
    1 tablespoon finely chopped scallion
    ¾ teaspoon salt
      Dash pepper
    1 tablespoon snipped fresh dill
    2 teaspoons lemon juice
    6 thin lemon slices

Combine buttermilk, cucumber, scallion, salt, pepper, dill and lemon juice. Chill. Garnish with lemon slices.

Cool Harvest Moon Soup

Makes 4 servings

    1½ cups boiling water
    2 teaspoons instant chicken bouillon
    1 can (10¾ ounces) condensed cream of chicken
      soup
    ½ cup Libby's Solid Pack Pumpkin
    ¼ cup half and half
      Dash celery salt
      Sour cream thinned with half and half
      Chopped chives

In blender container or food processor, dissolve bouillon in water; add soup, pumpkin, half and half, and celery salt. Cover; blend thoroughly. Chill. Stir before serving. Garnish with sour cream thinned with additional half and half so it will float on soup. Sprinkle with chives.

Note: Soup can be prepared in a bowl using a rotary beater or electric mixer.

Mexican Tomato Yogurt Soup

Makes 8 servings

- 1 tablespoon vegetable oil
- 4 cloves garlic
- 1 diced onion
- 1 teaspoon sugar
- 2 tablespoons chili powder
- 3 cups tomato purée
- 2 cups chicken broth
- 4 tablespoons canned diced green chili peppers
- 2 tablespoons cornstarch
- 2 cups Colombo Plain Yogurt
- 2 teaspoons salt (optional)
- 2 tablespoons green chili peppers, diced

Sauté garlic and onion in oil in a medium-size soup pan. Add sugar and chili powder. Add tomato purée and broth. Simmer 30 minutes. Mix chili peppers with cornstarch in a bowl; add to soup. Simmer 2 minutes; remove from heat. Put 1½ cups of yogurt into a bowl. Stir a ladle of soup into yogurt. Return yogurt mixture to pot, place over low heat, and stir gently. Taste and season with salt, if desired. Serve hot or cold. Fold a tablespoon of yogurt onto each plate; sprinkle with green chilis.

Soup's On
The size of a portion varies considerably, depending on the kind of soup you prepare and when you are serving it. A general rule of thumb about servings is to estimate one 8-ounce cup of soup per person if the soup is a first course and about 2 cups per serving if it is a main course.

Bloody Mary Soup

Makes about 7 servings

- 2 tablespoons oil
- 1 cup sliced onions
- 2 cups diced celery
- 1 can (1 quart 14 ounces) tomato juice
- 4 teaspoons sugar
- 1 teaspoon salt
- 1 tablespoon Lea & Perrins Worcestershire Sauce
- 1 tablespoon lemon juice
- ⅓ cup vodka

In a medium saucepan, heat oil. Add onions and celery; sauté for 3 minutes. Add tomato juice, sugar, salt, Lea & Perrins, and lemon juice. Bring to boiling point. Reduce heat and simmer uncovered for 10 minutes. Stir in vodka. Simmer uncovered 1 minute longer; strain. Cover and chill. Serve cold.

Yogurt-Potato Soup (page 17). Idaho Potato Commission

Gazpacho

Makes 6 to 7 servings

- 1 clove garlic, chopped
- 1 cucumber, peeled, seeded, and chopped
- 1 small green pepper, seeded and chopped
- ½ onion, chopped
- 2 ripe tomatoes, peeled, seeded, and chopped
- 2 cans (10¾ ounces each) Campbell's Condensed Tomato Soup
- 2 soup cans water
- 2 tablespoons olive oil
- ¼ cup lemon juice
- 1 teaspoon salt
  Dash Tabasco pepper sauce
  Croutons

Rub soup tureen with chopped garlic, then discard garlic. Put cucumber, green pepper, onion, and tomatoes in tureen. Mix tomato soup and water, and add to tureen with remaining ingredients. Chill until icy cold; serve sprinkled with tiny crisp croutons. Serve in bowls with an ice cube in each bowl.

Note: Gazpacho can be the main course of a light meal.

Mexican Tomato Yogurt Soup. Courtesy of Columbo, Inc.

Classic Gazpacho

Makes 6 servings
- ½ pound onions, peeled and quartered
- 6 tomatoes, peeled and quartered
- ½ cup red wine
- 2½ tablespoons olive oil
- 1 tablespoon paprika
- 1 clove garlic
- 1 cucumber, peeled, quartered, and thinly sliced
- 2 black olives, pitted and sliced
- Salt and pepper
- Finely chopped parsley
- Croutons

Combine onions, tomatoes, red wine, olive oil, paprika, and garlic clove. Place half in blender; cover and process at Purée until smooth. Empty into saucepan; repeat process with remaining half of mixture. Simmer 10 minutes. Stir the cucumber and olives into the soup, season to taste; chill. Sprinkle the soup liberally with finely chopped parsley and garnish with croutons.

Gazpacho with Currants

Makes 4 to 6 servings
- 3 large ripe tomatoes, peeled, seeded, and coarsely diced
- ½ small onion, cut up
- 1 clove garlic
- ¼ teaspoon cumin
- ¼ cup white wine vinegar or lemon juice
- 3 teaspoons olive oil
- ¾ teaspoon salt
- ½ cup water
- 1 large cucumber, peeled
- 1 large green pepper, seeded and diced
- ⅓ cup Sun-Maid® Zante Currants
- Croutons

Place the tomatoes, onion, garlic, cumin, vinegar, olive oil, salt, and water in a blender container or food processor and process until smooth. Cut the cucumber in half lengthwise and scoop out the seeds with the tip of a spoon. Cut the cucumber into chunks and add to the blender container with the green pepper. Turn blender on and off quickly to coarsely chop the cucumber and pepper. Add the currants and process just to mix. Correct the seasoning. Chill well before serving. Serve in chilled bowls garnished with croutons.

Icy Tomato-Buttermilk Soup

Makes about 4 cups
- 1 can (10¾ ounces) condensed tomato soup
- 2 medium-size tomatoes, diced
- 2 green onions, cut into 1-inch pieces
- 4 sprigs parsley
- 2 to 3 drops red pepper sauce
- 2 cups cold buttermilk
- ¼ cup diced celery

Place condensed soup, tomatoes, green onions, parsley, and pepper sauce in blender container; cover. Purée until tomatoes are finely chopped, about 15 seconds. Add buttermilk. Blend until well combined. Stir in celery by hand. Chill covered for 3 to 4 hours to allow flavors to blend.

Glorious Gazpacho

A tomato-based soup of Spanish origin, gazpacho has been with us for a long time—and with the Spaniards even longer.

Made with tomato juice, or better, puréed fresh tomatoes, gazpacho is flavored with onions, celery, and garlic, and often smoothed and mellowed with the addition of a little olive oil, and/or sharpened with wine or wine vinegar. The soup can be served hot, but it is almost always offered well chilled—a very refreshing part of the meal in hot weather. The usual method of making is to combine rather finely chopped vegetables with tomato juice, seasonings, and olive oil, and to allow the mixture to chill for several hours, during which the flavors will meld. This is often served over an ice cube or 2 in the soup dish.

A somewhat more attractive service, as well as a better-flavored soup, is achieved by puréeing peeled tomatoes, olive oil, red wine vinegar, celery, garlic, onion, and green pepper with salt and freshly ground pepper in the blender; this results in a liquid with more flavor and more body. Serve it in bowls or flat soup plates, accompanied by dishes of snipped parsley, thinly sliced green onions, crisp croutons, chopped celery, slivers of green pepper, and chopped cucumber, which each diner adds to his plate of soup in any combination and quantity he desires. Not strictly authentic, but good, are additions such as thin slices of raw cauliflower, mushrooms, and zucchini, and grated cheddar or Parmesan cheese. You can also offer wedges of lemon to sharpen the soup flavor for those who wish it, and hot pepper sauce to "heat" it.

Cold Curried Soup

Makes 8 servings

- 3 tablespoons butter
- 2 to 3 teaspoons curry powder
- 2 tablespoons all-purpose flour
- 4 cups chicken broth
- 3 egg yolks
- 1 cup light cream
- Snipped chives

Melt butter and stir in curry powder. Add the flour, stirring constantly. Slowly stir in chicken broth. Bring to a boil. Reduce heat. Beat together egg yolks and cream. Stir slowly into soup. Cook, stirring, over low heat until thickened slightly. Do not boil. Cool, then chill. Garnish with chives.

Chilled Curried Potato Soup

Makes 6 servings

- 2 tablespoons butter
- 1 tablespoon flour
- 2 teaspoons curry powder
- 1 can (10¼ ounces) Campbell's Condensed Cream of Potato Soup
- ½ cup sour cream
- 1 cup light cream

In a saucepan melt butter and stir in flour and curry. Add soup, sour cream, and light cream. Cook over low heat, stirring occasionally until soup is smooth and creamy. Cool and then chill. Serve in bowls set into crushed ice. Garnish with finely chopped walnuts and a little freshly grated coconut.

Beer Soup

Makes 4 servings

- 3 tablespoons sugar
- 2 tablespoons lemon juice
- 2 teaspoons ground cinnamon
- 2 cloves
- 1 teaspoon ground nutmeg
- 2 cups milk
- 2 tablespoons butter
- 2 tablespoons all-purpose flour
- 16 ounces beer
- 1 cup heavy cream

Place first 6 ingredients in heavy saucepot; heat to boiling, stirring constantly to avoid scorching sugar; remove from heat. Melt butter in another saucepan; stir in flour to form a paste. Return milk mixture to heat and stir in butter-flour paste; stir with a wire whisk until desired soup consistency is reached (soup should coat the outside of a spoon). Add beer and cream. Chill thoroughly. Remove cloves before serving.

Cold Swiss Chard Soup

Makes 6 servings

- 1 bunch Swiss chard, chopped
- ½ cup chopped celery
- 4 green onions, chopped
- 2 tablespoons fresh parsley
- 1 clove garlic, minced
- ⅛ teaspoon *each* oregano, dill weed, and pepper
- 2 chicken bouillon cubes
- 2 tablespoons olive oil
- 2 cups water
- 1 cup Paul Masson Chablis
- 3 tablespoons grated Parmesan cheese

Simmer Swiss chard, celery, onions, parsley, garlic, seasonings, bouillon cubes, oil, and water 20 minutes; add wine. Heat 10 more minutes. Blend soup in food processor or blender until puréed; blend in cheese. Chill.

Chilled Cream of Zucchini Soup

Makes 4 servings

- 2 tablespoons butter
- 2 tablespoons onion, chopped
- 2 tablespoons parsley, snipped
- 1 tablespoon dill, snipped
- Salt and pepper to taste
- 2 cups milk
- 1 large zucchini
- 1 cup sour cream

Melt butter in large saucepot; add onion, parsley, dill, salt, and pepper, and sauté until onion is wilted. Add milk, and cook, stirring constantly, until soup thickens, about 15 minutes. Slice zucchini thinly and add to soup, reserving a few slices for garnish. Cook until zucchini is tender, about 10 minutes. Pour soup into blender and process on purée until smooth. Stir in sour cream while soup is still hot. Chill completely; garnish with reserved zucchini slices.

Chilly Summertime Refresher

Light soups and summertime are a match made in heaven! Soups cap off the season like no other food on the menu—they're soothing, refreshing, and filling. To keep frosty soups as cold as possible, chill mugs, cups, sherbet dishes, or bowls in the freezer before serving.

Cold soups are a pleasing complement to a sandwich or summer salad menu, or a light supper on a sultry evening. They're also quick-to-prepare camping fare, or tasty picnic or office lunches when stored in a wide-mouthed thermos.

Fruits 'n' Nuts

What are some of the soup-erlatives you'll hear when you set forth one of these surprises? "Imaginative! Unexpected! Encore!"

Orange Cantaloupe Soup

Makes 4 servings
- 1 large cantaloupe
- 2 cups water, divided
- 1 can (6 ounces) undiluted Florida frozen concentrated orange juice, thawed
- ½ teaspoon salt
- ⅛ teaspoon ground cinnamon
  Dash mace
- 2 tablespoons cornstarch

Cut cantaloupe in half and remove seeds. Using a melon-ball scoop, scoop balls from one half; set aside. Scrape out pulp; reserve. Peel remaining half; cut into chunks. Place cantaloupe chunks and pulp in container of electric blender; cover; process until smooth. (You should have 1 cup purée.) Add 1 cup water, concentrated orange juice, salt, cinnamon, and mace. Cover. Process 5 seconds. In small saucepan, combine cornstarch and remaining 1 cup water; stir to dissolve cornstarch. Cook over medium heat until mixture boils and thickens; gently stir into cantaloupe mixture. Add melon balls. Chill before serving.

Danish Buttermilk Soup

Makes 4 servings
- 6 egg yolks
- ¼ cup sugar
- 1 quart buttermilk
- 6 tablespoons (½ of 6-ounce can) undiluted Florida frozen concentrated grapefruit juice, thawed

In large bowl of electric mixer, beat egg yolks and sugar until thick and lemon colored. Gently stir in buttermilk and grapefruit juice concentrate. Chill.

Orange Raspberry Soup

Makes 4 servings
- 2 cups light cream or half and half
- 1 package (10 ounces) frozen raspberries, thawed
- 1 can (6 ounces) undiluted Florida frozen concentrated orange juice, thawed
- ½ cup heavy cream, whipped
  Grated orange rind (optional)

In container of electric blender, combine light cream, raspberries, and concentrated orange juice. Cover. Process on high 1 minute until smooth. Chill. Garnish with whipped cream. Sprinkle with grated orange rind, if desired.

Sunshine Avocado Soup

Makes 4 servings
- 2 cups light cream or half and half
- 1¼ cups water
- 1 can (6 ounces) undiluted Florida frozen concentrated orange juice, thawed
- 2 ripe avocados
- ½ teaspoon salt
- ⅛ teaspoon hot pepper sauce
  Orange slices (optional)

In container of electric blender, combine light cream, water, and concentrated orange juice. Process until smooth. Peel and seed avocados. Cut 1½ avocados into chunks. Add to blender with salt and hot pepper sauce. Blend 1 minute until smooth. Chill. Cut remaining avocado half into slices. Garnish soup with avocado and orange slices.

Orange Cantaloupe Soup; Danish Buttermilk Soup; Orange Raspberry Soup; Sunshine Avocado Soup. **Florida Department of Citrus**

Cold Fruit Soup

Makes 8 servings
    1 can (6 ounces) frozen lemonade concentrate
    2 lemonade cans plus 2 tablespoons cold water
    1 can (12 ounces) apricot nectar
    ½ cup Sun-Maid® Dried Apricots
    ⅓ cup Sun-Maid® Seedless Raisins
    2 tablespoons sugar
    1 3-inch stick cinnamon
    3 whole allspice or cloves
    2 tablespoons cornstarch
    1 bag (20 ounces) frozen mixed fruit, partially
        thawed
      Sour cream

Mix the lemonade concentrate with water in a 3-quart saucepan. Add the apricot nectar, apricots, raisins, sugar, cinnamon, and allspice. Bring to a boil, stirring once. Reduce heat and simmer uncovered for 5 minutes. Dissolve the cornstarch in 2 tablespoons cold water and stir into the soup; cook until the mixture boils and thickens. Remove from the heat and cool for 15 minutes before stirring in the frozen fruit. Refrigerate until well chilled. Serve with dollop of sour cream.

Sherried Apple-Fruit Soup

Makes about 2 quarts
    1 quart water
    1 package (11 ounces) mixed dried fruit
    3 large apples
    ½ cup sugar
    3 tablespoons tapioca
    ¼ cup dry sherry

Pour water in large saucepan. Add dried fruit to water, cutting larger pieces in half. Cover saucepan and bring to boil; reduce heat and simmer 10 minutes. Peel, core, and cut apples in eighths; add to cooked fruit and simmer 10 minutes longer. Stir in sugar and tapioca, cooking until mixture is clear and thickened. Remove from heat and add sherry. Serve warm as a soup or chilled as a dessert or ice cream topping. Fruit thickens when refrigerated and will keep indefinitely.

Chilled Avocado Soup

Makes about 4½ cups
    1 tablespoon instant chicken bouillon
    1 cup boiling water
    ⅛ teaspoon pepper
    1 thin slice (⅛ inch thick) unpeeled lemon,
        quartered
    1 thin slice (⅛ inch thick) onion, halved
  2½ cups milk
    2 cups peeled diced avocado
      Corn chips

Place bouillon, water, pepper, lemon, and onion in blender container; cover. Grate until fairly smooth, about 30 seconds. Add milk and avocado. Grate until smooth, about 1 minute. Chill covered 3 to 4 hours to allow flavors to blend. Serve with corn chips.

Cold Monterey Avocado Soup

Makes 6 to 8 servings
    3 cups light cream
    1 can (10½ ounces) Campbell's Condensed
        Cream of Chicken Soup
      Dash Worcestershire sauce
    ½ teaspoon salt
    ¼ teaspoon pepper
      Sprinkle ground nutmeg
    2 ripe medium-size avocados
      Chopped chives

Mix together all ingredients except avocados and chill well. Just before serving, peel avocados and remove seeds. Press through a sieve or whirl in a blender. Stir in previously mixed and chilled ingredients and blend well. Serve garnished with chopped chives.

Binding and Thickening Soup

Flour is often used in soups to add body and inhibit curdling or separation. The correct proportion for 2 cups of soup is 1 tablespoon melted butter to 1 tablespoon flour. Stir flour into butter and cook it about 3 minutes over low heat; stir in a little hot soup, whisk well, cook until thick, then add to remaining soup. Heat and stir until smooth.

Egg yolks are also used to thicken soups: 1 egg yolk beaten with 1 teaspoon milk or cream to each cup of soup—added just before serving. To prevent curdling, drizzle a little hot soup slowly into egg yolks, whisk briefly, pour into soup pot, and reheat slowly, stirring until it thickens. Be careful not to boil because the eggs will curdle.

Cherry Soup

Makes 6 servings

  1 pound dark sweet cherries, pitted
  1 cup dry red wine
  1 lemon, sliced and seeded
  1 stick cinnamon
  3 tablespoons sugar
  2 tablespoons cornstarch
  2 tablespoons lemon juice
    Lemon slices
    Sour cream

Microwave: Combine cherries, wine, sliced lemon, and cinnamon stick in 2½-quart glass bowl or casserole. Cover tightly with Saran Wrap, turning back edge to vent. Microcook at 100% power 7 minutes. Stir, recover, leaving vent, and microcook at 50% power 10 minutes. Cool slightly. Pour about half the mixture into blender or food processor. Blend until smooth. Transfer to bowl. Repeat with remaining cherry mixture. Mix sugar and cornstarch. Stir into cherry mixture. Cover tightly with Saran Wrap, turning back edge to vent. Microcook at 100% power 8 minutes, or until mixture boils, stirring 2 or 3 times. Add lemon juice and chill. Top servings with lemon slices and a dollop of sour cream.

Conventional: Combine cherries, wine, sliced lemon, and cinnamon stick in 2-quart saucepan. Heat to boiling. Reduce heat, cover and simmer 20 minutes, stirring occasionally. Blend mixture as in microwave method, then return soup to saucepan. Combine sugar and cornstarch and stir into soup. Bring to full rolling boil. Boil 1 minute. Add lemon juice and chill. Top servings with lemon slices and a dollop of sour cream.

Lemon Soup

Makes 6 servings

  2 cans (10½ ounces each) Campbell's Condensed
    Chicken Broth
  2 soup cans water
  1 cup raw vermicelli, broken into 3-inch lengths
  3 eggs, well beaten
  ½ cup lemon juice
    Salt and pepper

In a large saucepan, combine chicken broth and water. Bring to a boil; add vermicelli and cook until vermicelli is tender. Beat eggs with lemon juice. Gradually beat in some of the hot soup. Beat this mixture into the remaining soup. Reheat but do not boil. Season to taste with salt and pepper.

Chilled Kiwi Soup

Makes 4¾ cups

  2 ripe kiwi fruit, peeled and sliced (reserve 4
    slices for garnish)
  2 packets (½ teaspoon) Sweet 'N Low® granulated
    sugar substitute, divided
  1 tablespoon margarine
  ½ leek (white only), thinly sliced
  1 small red potato, peeled and thinly sliced
  2 cups chicken consommé
  1 mint leaf
    Salt, white pepper to taste
  ¼ cup plain low-fat yogurt

Sprinkle sliced kiwi with 1 packet Sweet 'N Low. Cover; chill overnight. In saucepan, melt margarine. Add kiwi, leek, potato, comsommé, 1 packet Sweet 'N Low, and mint leaf; simmer 6 to 8 minutes. Adjust seasoning, if desired. In blender, purée mixture. Chill about 1 hour, or until mixture coats a spoon thickly; add yogurt and purée again. Serve in chilled soup cups. Float reserved kiwi slices on top.

Peanut-Tomato Soup

Makes about 4 servings

  2 cans (10¾ ounces each) condensed tomato soup
  ¼ cup peanut butter
  ¼ teaspoon basil
  2 soup cans milk

Blend soup, peanut butter, and basil in saucepan. Add milk gradually, stirring until evenly blended. Heat to serving temperature.

Orange Fruit Soup

Makes 8 to 10 servings

  3 cans (16 ounces each) pears, drained
  6 cups Florida orange juice
  1½ teaspoons ground cardamom
  ¾ cup sour cream
  5 Florida oranges, peeled and sectioned
    Assorted garnishes: crème fraîche, toasted
      coconut, avocado slices, macadamia nuts,
      orange and grapefruit sections

Purée pears in blender until smooth. (This may be done in several batches.) Pour purée into a bowl. Stir in orange juice, cardamom, and sour cream. Chill. Add orange sections. Serve with assorted garnishes.

Potato-Almond Soup. Campbell Soup Company

Potato-Almond Soup

Makes 4 to 5 servings

>   1 can (10½ ounces) Campbell's Condensed
>   Cream of Potato Soup
> 1½ soup cans half and half
>   ½ cup toasted slivered almonds
>   1 can (10½ ounces) Campbell's Condensed
>   Chicken Broth
>   Dash pepper
>   Snipped chives, watercress, or parsley

Combine cream of potato soup, half and half, and almonds in a blender container. Blend until smooth. Pour into a saucepan; add chicken broth and pepper. Heat, stirring occasionally. Serve hot, garnished with snipped chives, watercress, or parsley.

Cream of Almond Soup

Makes 6 servings

>   1 cup blanched almonds
>   2 tablespoons chopped onion
>   ¼ cup chopped celery
> 1½ tablespoons butter
> 1½ tablespoons all-purpose flour
>   1 can (10½ ounces) Campbell's Condensed
>   Cream of Chicken Soup
>   1 soup can water
>   1 cup light cream
>   ¼ teaspoon white pepper
>   ½ teaspoon salt
>   ½ teaspoon almond extract
>   Slivered toasted almonds (optional)

Toast almonds by heating them in a small skillet over medium heat. Stir occasionally. Grind almonds very fine. Sauté onion and celery in butter until golden. Stir in flour. Stir in cream of chicken soup, water, light cream, pepper, and salt. Add almonds. Simmer for 20 minutes, stirring occasionally. Stir in almond extract. Can be served hot or cold, topped with slivered toasted almonds.

Raisin-Peanut Soup

Makes 4 to 6 servings

>   1 can (10¾ ounces) condensed chicken broth,
>   undiluted
>   1 soup can half and half or milk
>   ½ cup creamy or chunky peanut butter
>   ⅓ cup Sun-Maid® Seedless Golden Raisins,
>   chopped
>   ⅛ teaspoon salt
>   5 to 10 drops hot pepper sauce
>   1 tablespoon medium-dry sherry
>   Sliced scallions

Heat the chicken broth with the half and half until bubbles form around the edges of the saucepan. Add the peanut butter, whisking until smooth, then stir in the remaining ingredients except scallions. Serve warm or chilled. Garnish with sliced scallions.

Q. *Two terms that often come up in soup recipes are* thicken *and* reduce. *What do they mean, what is their purpose, and how are they accomplished?*

A. Reduce. Make the volume of a liquid less; *purpose:* to concentrate flavor and/or thicken the liquid slightly; *method:* over heat, by boiling or simmering uncovered—reduction is effected by evaporation.

Thicken. Add starch to liquid to make it denser; *purpose:* to produce a sauce or gravy that will cling to food, rather than running, as a liquid does—also, sometimes, in doing so to incorporate other ingredients such as butter or cream to enrich the sauce; *method:* (a) combine flour, cornstarch, arrowroot, or other thickening agent with cold liquid (water, broth, milk, cream), add gradually to hot soup, stew, or sauce, stirring constantly, (b) knead together equal amounts of butter and flour, add in bits to hot mixture while stirring (this is beurre manié), or (c) melt fat, stir in flour, and cook briefly before adding liquid (this is a roux).

Cherry Soup (page 25). Photograph is compliments of Saran Wrap™ brand plastic film

Creole-Style Peanut Soup

Makes about 5½ cups
- ½ cup butter
- 1 cup chopped peanuts
- 1 cup chopped carrots
- ½ cup chopped celery
- ¼ cup chopped green onion
- 1 clove garlic, crushed
- ¼ cup all-purpose flour
- 2 cans (13¾ ounces each) chicken broth
- 1 cup milk
  Chopped parsley

Melt butter in saucepan over medium heat. Add peanuts, carrots, celery, onion, and garlic. Sauté vegetables until tender. Blend in flour; gradually stir in broth. Simmer 15 minutes to blend flavors. Stir in milk; heat to serving temperature. Garnish with parsley.

Curried Raisin-Yogurt Soup

Makes 6 servings
- 1 cup chopped carrots
- 1 medium-size onion, chopped
- 1 teaspoon curry powder
- ¼ cup butter or margarine
- ⅓ cup Sun-Maid® Seedless Golden Raisins
- ½ teaspoon salt
- 1 can (10¾ ounces) condensed chicken broth, undiluted
- 2 cups plain yogurt, at room temperature
  Shredded cucumber

Sauté carrots, onion, and curry powder in butter until the onion is soft but not browned. Stir in raisins, salt, and chicken broth and bring to a boil. Reduce heat, cover, and simmer for 10 minutes. Pour carrot mixture into a blender container or food processor and process until smooth. Add the yogurt and process just until mixed. Pour into individual bowls and serve immediately garnished with shredded cucumber. (This soup is best eaten at the temperature it ends up—warm.)

Fruit Soup

Makes 4 cups
- 1 pound cherries, pitted
- 2 cups water
- 1 cup red wine
- ¼ cup Sue Bee Honey
- ½ teaspoon grated orange rind
- 1 teaspoon arrowroot
  Unsweetened whipped cream (optional)

Put cherries in an enamel pan and cover with water, wine, Sue Bee Honey, and orange rind. Cook until cherries are soft, about 10 minutes. Blend or sieve cherries, and thicken juice with arrowroot mixed with a little of the cooked syrup. Return mixture to the soup and cook about 2 minutes. Serve hot or cold. Garnish with unsweetened whipped cream, if desired.

April Dew

Makes 6 servings
- ½ cantaloupe, peeled and seeded
- 1 pear, peeled and cored
- 1 can (8 ounces) cling peaches, drained
  Juice of ½ lime
- 1½ teaspoons sugar
  Salt, coarse pepper to taste
- 1¼ cups chilled Paul Masson Rosé
  Rose petals

Blend fruit juice, sugar, salt, and pepper in a blender and refrigerate 3 hours. Just before serving add Rosé and pour into balloon glasses. Garnish with rose petals.

Strawberry Soup with Apple Marmalade

Makes four ¾-cup servings★
- 1 bottle dry white wine
- 5 mint leaves, divided
- 4 vanilla beans, divided
- 7 packets (2¼ teaspoons) Sweet 'N Low® granulated sugar substitute, divided
- 2 tart cooking apples (such as Rome Beauty or Jonathan), peeled, cored, and thinly sliced
- 2 sweet eating apples (such as Red Delicious or McIntosh), peeled, cored, and thinly sliced
- 1 tablespoon water
- ½ pint fresh strawberries, sliced

In saucepan, heat wine, 1 mint leaf, 3 vanilla beans and 3 packets Sweet 'N Low about 20 minutes, or until there is about 1 cup liquid. Chill about 2 hours. Remove vanilla beans and mint leaf. Meanwhile, in another saucepan, combine apple slices, 4 packets Sweet 'N Low, 1 tablespoon water, and 1 vanilla bean; heat about 15 minutes. Chill about 1½ hours. Discard vanilla bean. To serve, spoon a layer of apple mixture in bottom of soup cup. Arrange strawberries on top. At the last moment, pour wine mixture over fruit. Garnish with mint leaves.

★You can save about 125 calories per serving with this Sweet 'N Low recipe.

Chilled Avocado-Yogurt Soup

Makes 6 servings

    2 California avocados, seeded and peeled
    2 teaspoons lemon juice
    2 cups chicken broth or bouillon
    ½ teaspoon onion
       salt
    ½ teaspoon celery salt
    1 carton (16 ounces) plain low-fat yogurt
       Additional plain low-fat yogurt
    1 tablespoon chopped chives.

Place avocados, lemon juice, chicken broth, season-ings, and yogurt in blender jar; whir until smooth. Chill soup thoroughly. Garnish each serving with a dollop of additional stirred yogurt and chopped chives.

Golden Fruit Soup

Makes 5 to 6 servings

    1 package (11 ounces) mixed dried fruit
    2 cups orange juice
    1 cup water
    ½ lemon, thinly sliced
    1½ tablespoons tapioca
    ¼ teaspoon salt
    ½ cup Domino Liquid Brown Sugar
    1 stick cinnamon
   10 whole cloves

Cut up large pieces of dried fruit. In saucepan, com-bine fruit with remaining ingredients. Cover and simmer 20 to 25 minutes, or until fruit is tender. Cool. Serve well chilled.

Orange-Lime Soup

Makes 5 or 6 servings

    2½ tablespoons cornstarch
    ¼ cup sugar
    4 cups orange juice
    5 or 6 thin slices lime
       Sour cream
       Cinnamon

Combine cornstarch and sugar in saucepan. Stir in 1 cup orange juice and mix until smooth. Cook over moderate heat, stirring constantly, until mixture thick-ens and clears. Remove from heat and cool slightly. Gradually beat in remaining orange juice. Chill. Garnish with slice of lime topped with sour cream and a dash of cinnamon.

Avocado Buttermilk Soup

Makes 6 servings

    2 teaspoons low-sodium chicken-flavor bouillon
       mix or 2 cubes low-sodium chicken-flavor
       bouillon
    ½ cup boiling water
       Ice and water to make 1 cup
    1 slice medium onion, ½ inch thick
    ¼ teaspoon celery seed
    1⅓ cups mashed ripe California avocado
    2 to 4 tablespoons fresh lemon juice
    1 cup unsalted buttermilk
    ½ cup plain low-fat yogurt
       Lemon wedges or slices
       Minced green onion tops or parsley

Dissolve chicken-flavor bouillon mix or cubes in boil-ing water; stir in ice water. Combine bouillon, onion, celery seed, avocado, and 2 tablespoons lemon juice in blender jar. Blend until avocado is completely smooth; pour into a 6-cup bowl or pitcher. Whisk buttermilk and yogurt into avocado mixture. Add additional lemon juice to taste. Place plastic wrap directly on surface of soup and chill thoroughly. Serve in cold mugs or icers; garnish with lemon and green onion or parsley.

All About Avocados

How to buy and store. Avocados are picked and shipped when under-mature because, unlike many fruits, they ripen best off the tree. If you want to use the fruit the day or the day after you buy it, you may be hard put to it to find one ripe enough, unless you search out a gourmet market. Avocado lovers under-stand that they must wait a while for ripeness, and generally bring home immature fruit to store at room temperature until they have ripened.

For immediate use, choose avocados that yield to gentle pressure when cradled between the palms of your hands. Or buy fruit that is uniformly hard to ripen at home.

Tips on preparing, cooking. To halve an avocado, cut it all around, pit deep, from stem to stern. Hold-ing between your hands, twist the halves gently in opposite directions until they come apart. Spear the pit with the tip of your knife to remove it. To peel, start with a sharp knife, peel off the skin—if the avocado is properly ripe, it will come off readily.

In cooking avocado, be gentle and wary. Brief cooking at low temperature enhances flavor, but long cooking at high heat is ruinous to the avocado's deli-cate texture. Use a stainless knife to prepare avocado, and brush cut surfaces with lemon juice, a weak (1 tablespoon to 2 cups water) vinegar solution, or an ascorbic acid mixture (follow package directions) to prevent discoloration. Add one of these aids against discoloration to mashed or puréed avocado, too.

Hearty Chowders and Vegetable Soups

Rich and rib-sticking, these earthy and wholesome main dishes are always as welcoming as a warm hearth.

Fresh Summer Vegetable Soup

Makes 6 servings

    4 cups chicken broth
    1 carrot, sliced
    1 onion, diced
    2 sprigs parsley
    ¼ teaspoon oregano
    2 ears corn, or 1 can (8 ounces) whole-kernel
        corn, drained
 1½ cups cauliflowerets (about ¼ medium-size
        head)
    1 cup fresh green beans, cut into 1-inch pieces
    1 medium-size zucchini, sliced
    2 tomatoes, cut into chunks
      Salt and freshly ground pepper to taste
      Chopped parsley

Microwave: Combine chicken broth, carrot, onion, parsley, and oregano in 3-quart microsafe soup tureen or casserole. Cover tightly with Saran Wrap, turning back edge to vent. Microcook at 100% power 6 minutes. Cut kernels from ears of corn. Add corn, cauliflower, and green beans to soup. Recover, leaving vent, and microcook at 100% power 10 minutes. Add zucchini and tomatoes. Recover and microcook at 100% power 5 minutes. Season to taste with salt and pepper. Ladle into soup bowls and sprinkle with chopped parsley.

Conventional: Combine chicken broth, carrot, onion, parsley, and oregano in large saucepan. Heat to boiling. Reduce heat, cover, and simmer 10 minutes. Cut kernels from ears of corn. Add corn, cauliflower, and green beans to soup. Cover and simmer 12 minutes. Stir in zucchini and tomatoes and simmer 5 minutes. Season to taste with salt and pepper. Serve as above.

Nice to know: A handful of chopped fresh spinach, stirred into steaming soup just before serving, adds extra nourishment and flavor.

San Francisco Minestrone

Makes 6 to 8 servings

    ¼ pound salt pork or chunk bacon
    1 medium onion, chopped
    1 clove garlic, minced
    5 cups water and 1 cup meat stock, or 6 cups
        water and 2 bouillon cubes
    1 cup dry large lima beans
    1 teaspoon salt
    1 carrot, sliced
    1 turnip, halved and sliced
    2 cups sliced celery
    ½ bay leaf
    ¼ teaspoon dried basil
 1½ cup canned stewed tomatoes
    1 cup chopped spinach
    2 cups shredded cabbage
    ¼ cup uncooked rice
      Grated Parmesan or Romano cheese

Cut pork in cubes and fry with onion and garlic until lightly browned. Put water and meat stock in a large soup kettle. Add washed dry limas and the browned pork mixture, and bring to a boil. Next add salt, carrot, turnip, celery, bay leaf, and basil, and boil gently for 1½ hours. Add tomatoes, spinach, cabbage, and rice, and cook ½ hour longer, until rice is done. Taste, add additional salt if needed. Serve in tureen. Ladle into individual bowls, with grated cheese on top.

> **Q.** *Can soups be frozen?*
> **A.** Soups such as onion, chicken noodle, split pea, navy bean, and vegetable freeze well, as do chowders. Meat and chicken stocks and vegetable purées may also be frozen for later use as the basis for soups. When preparing soups for freezing, cool quickly by immersing container in ice water. When packaging soups and other liquids, be sure to leave at least 1 inch of headspace in the container to allow for expansion.

Calico Corn Chowder (page 33); Split Pea and Ham Soup (page 34).
Courtesy of Geo. A. Hormel & Co.

Wintry Vegetable Soup

Makes 10 servings

    6 slices bacon, chopped
    3 leeks, white part only, cleaned and thinly sliced
    3 carrots, peeled and chopped
    2 stalks celery, chopped
    2 parsnips, peeled and chopped
    1 large onion, finely chopped
2½ quarts chicken stock
    1 pound dried white beans, soaked in water
        overnight
    1 jar (15½ ounces) Ragú Homestyle Spaghetti
        Sauce
    2 smoked ham hocks or ham bones
    1 bay leaf
    1 teaspoon thyme
  ¼ teaspoon pepper
    Salt to taste
    Chopped fresh parsley

In a large saucepan or stockpot, cook bacon until crisp. Remove bacon and set aside. In the same saucepan, sauté leeks, carrots, celery, parsnips, and onion in bacon drippings until vegetables are tender. Return bacon to pan; add chicken stock, beans, spaghetti sauce, ham hocks, bay leaf, thyme, pepper, and salt. Bring to a boil; reduce heat and simmer covered 2 hours, or until beans are tender. Remove ham hocks; trim meat from bones and return meat to soup. Discard bay leaf. Serve soup with parsley.

Homestyle Minestrone Soup

Makes 12 servings

    9 cups water
    9 cups beef stock
    1 jar (48 ounces) Ragú Homestyle Spaghetti
        Sauce
4½ cups thinly sliced carrots
2¼ cups finely chopped onions
1½ cups chopped celery
    2 tablespoons minced fresh parsley
    1 tablespoon basil
    2 small bay leaves
    Salt to taste
    Pepper to taste
    3 cups frozen peas
    3 cups ditalini, cooked and drained
    Grated Parmesan cheese

In a large saucepan or stockpot, combine first 11 ingredients; simmer 45 minutes, stirring occasionally. Add peas and ditalini; simmer 20 minutes, or until vegetables are tender. Discard bay leaves. Serve soup with cheese.

Tomato Soup Tips

If a recipe calls for cut-up canned tomatoes, save yourself messy cleanup and cut them in the can. A sharp knife or kitchen shears will do the job. Either insert the knife into the can and cut the tomatoes against the sides or simply cut the tomatoes with the shears. Don't worry about draining the tomatoes; usually your recipe will call for adding both the tomatoes and their juices.

If you prefer fresh tomatoes and "fresh" tomato soup but think you can't have them all year long, reconsider. When fresh tomatoes are at their most abundant (and least expensive), make concentrated tomato soup base, freeze it, thin with milk or light cream when you heat, and eat—even on a winter's day.

Chunks of Tomato Soup

Makes 6 cups

3½ cups (28-ounce can) Contadina® Peeled Whole
        Tomatoes and juice
  ¼ cup instant minced onion
    2 tablespoons chopped parsley
    2 teaspoons sugar
    1 teaspoon cumin
  ½ teaspoon salt
  ¼ teaspoon pepper
  ¼ cup butter
  ¼ cup all-purpose flour
1½ cups undiluted Carnation® Evaporated Milk
    1 cup water
    Cilantro Pesto (recipe follows)

Cut up tomatoes. Combine tomatoes, juice, onion, parsley, sugar, cumin, salt, and pepper in medium bowl. Melt butter in large saucepan. Stir in flour until well blended. Gradually stir in evaporated milk and water. Cook over medium heat, stirring constantly, until mixture just comes to a boil. Stir in tomato mixture; heat just to serving temperature. Serve with Cilantro Pesto.

Cilantro Pesto

Makes 1 cup

    2 cups fresh Cilantro
    1 clove garlic
  ½ cup grated Parmesan cheese
    2 tablespoons oil
  ½ cup toasted sesame seed

Process cilantro and garlic in blender or food processor until finely chopped. Add Parmesan cheese and oil. Process to a smooth paste. Stir in toasted sesame seed.

Calico Corn Chowder

Makes 1½ quarts

- ½ cup chopped onion
- ½ cup chopped green pepper
- 1 tablespoon butter or margarine
- 2 cans (1 pound each) cream-style corn
- 2 cups milk
- 1 can (7 ounces) SPAM® Luncheon Meat, diced
- ¼ teaspoon garlic salt
  Pepper to taste

In medium saucepan, sauté onion and green pepper in butter until vegetables are tender but not browned. Add corn, milk, SPAM®, garlic salt, and pepper; bring to a boil over medium heat, stirring often. Lower heat; simmer 10 minutes.

Italian Vegetable Soup

Makes 6 to 8 servings

- 2 cans (10½ ounces each) condensed beef consommé
- 3½ cups water
- ½ cup lentils, rinsed
- 3 bacon slices, diced
- 1 can (8 ounces) tomato sauce
- 1 package (1½ ounces) Lawry's Spaghetti Sauce Seasoning Blend with Imported Mushrooms
- 2 cloves garlic
- ½ teaspoon Lawry's Seasoned Salt
- ½ teaspoon Lawry's Seasoned Pepper
- ½ cup coarsely shredded cabbage
- ½ cup uncooked elbow macaroni (smallest size)
- 1 package (10 ounces) frozen mixed vegetables
- 2 tablespoons finely chopped parsley
  French or Italian bread (optional)

In Dutch oven, place consommé, water, lentils, and bacon. Bring to a boil; reduce heat and simmer covered 1 hour. Add tomato sauce and Spaghetti Sauce Seasoning Blend with Imported Mushrooms; blend well. Insert toothpick into each garlic clove; add to soup with Seasoned Salt, Seasoned Pepper, and cabbage. Simmer 25 minutes. Bring soup to a boil; add macaroni, vegetables, and parsley; blend well. Simmer about 10 minutes, or until macaroni is tender. Remove garlic. Serve with crusty French or Italian bread.

Stock Report

Simply stated, stock is water transformed by the glorious things that have been cooked in it: garden-fresh vegetables; bones, scraps, and cuts of meat, poultry, and fish; herbs and spices. Stock is the basic ingredient to many soups and sauces.

Ingredients for stock are as varied as your kitchen shelf is from that of your neighbor. Staples, however, include onions, celery, bay leaves, peppercorns, and cloves; meat bones; poultry skin, carcasses, and giblets; fish heads and skeletons; leftover meat, chicken, and fish scraps; cooked vegetables; mushroom stems, celery tops, parsley stems. All these can be refrigerated or frozen until you are ready to use them in the stockpot. Take care to avoid smoked or corned meats, cabbage, turnips, and dark oily fish. Their tastes may be too strong or make the stock too salty.

When you are ready to prepare the stock, assemble your ingredients and keep in mind a few pointers:

- Before adding vegetables to stock, wash and cut them up. Since they will be strained out later, there's no need to peel or trim them.
- Start with cold water to get the maximum flavor from your meats and vegetables. Cold water extracts the juices and mingles them with the water.
- Always simmer stocks—just a bubble or 2 that burst the surface. Skim off any scum that rises to the surface during the first half hour. Once the scum becomes a white froth, it will disappear by itself.
- Partially cover stockpot during simmering in order to maintain simmer and reduce liquid somewhat.
- Cooking times vary according to kind of stock: Fish or vegetable stocks should not cook longer than 30 minutes or they may become bitter; meat or poultry stocks should simmer all day—or as long as possible.
- Strain the stock through a colander lined with cheesecloth and let it cool uncovered as quickly as possible—in the refrigerator or other similarly cold place.
- When stock is cold, fat will have formed on the surface. Do not remove until ready to use the stock. To remove, lift or spoon off.
- To keep stock from spoiling, freeze or store in refrigerator. If stored in the refrigerator, stock should be reheated every 3 days and allowed to boil 2 minutes. Return to refrigerator. If you add any additional juice or gravy to the stock, stock must also be boiled again.

Double Pea Soup

Makes 8 servings

  1 can (1 pound 4 ounces) chick peas
    Water
  1 can (11¼ ounces) condensed green pea soup
  1 can (10¾ ounces) condensed cream of chicken
    soup
  1 tablespoon Lea & Perrins Worcestershire Sauce
  1 teaspoon basil leaves, crumbled
  ¼ cup chopped parsley

Drain chick peas, reserving liquid and peas separately. To chick pea liquid add sufficient water to measure 2½ cups. In a saucepan, combine chick pea liquid and pea soup; mix well. Stir in chicken soup, Lea & Perrins, basil, and reserved chick peas. Bring to boiling point, stirring occasionally. Add parsley and serve hot.

Split Pea and Ham Soup

Makes 2 quarts

  1 cup (½ pound) split green peas
  1 cup peeled and diced potatoes
  ½ cup diced carrots
  ½ cup chopped celery
  1 medium onion, chopped
  6 cups water
1½ teaspoons salt, divided
  ¼ teaspoon pepper
  1 can (6¾ ounces) Hormel Chunk Ham
  1 large clove garlic

In large saucepan, combine split peas, potatoes, carrots, celery, onion, water, ½ teaspoon salt, and pepper. Drain liquid from ham into saucepan. Coarsely chop ham; add to saucepan. Bring to boil; simmer covered 1 hour. Crush garlic with remaining 1 teaspoon salt; stir into soup. Cover and simmer 30 minutes longer.

San Francisco Minestrone (page 31). Gordon E. Smith

Potato-Tomato Bisque; Fish-Potato Chowder (page 41). Wisconsin Potato Growers Auxiliary

Fresh Summer Vegetable Soup (page 31). Photograph is compliments of Saran Wrap™ brand plastic film

Potato-Tomato Bisque

Makes 6 to 8 servings

- ½ cup butter or margarine
- 1 medium onion, thinly sliced
- 4 cups peeled, chopped ripe tomatoes
- 1 cup tomato juice
- 3 medium potatoes, washed, peeled, and sliced (3 cups)
- ½ teaspoon salt
- ½ teaspoon tarragon
- ¼ teaspoon rosemary
- ⅛ teaspoon white pepper
- 2 cups half and half, heated
  - Minced parsley or chives

Melt butter in 3-quart saucepan. Sauté onion until transparent; do not brown. Add tomatoes and tomato juice; simmer until tomatoes are soft. Add potatoes, salt, tarragon, rosemary, and pepper. Simmer about 30 minutes, or until potatoes are tender, stirring occasionally. Remove from heat; cool slightly. Place mixture, 2 cups at a time, in bowl of food processor or blender container; purée. Return purée to saucepan; stir in half and half. Sprinkle parsley or chives on each serving.

Q. *We're a family of dumpling-eaters—in soups and stews, and sweet ones cooked in a fruit sauce. Is there any way to get the dumpling batter to fall off the spoon in neat, even pieces?*

A. Easy. Before spooning out each dumpling, dip the spoon into the hot liquid—the soup, stew, or fruit syrup.

Russian Hill Bean Borscht

Makes 6 to 8 cups

- 2 large raw beets
- 1 medium onion
- 7 to 8 cups strong clear beef broth
- 1 to 1½ cups cooked or canned California pink or red kidney beans
- 2 cups shredded cabbage
- 1 tablespoon butter
- 1 tablespoon lemon juice
  - Salt and pepper to taste
  - Sour cream

Wash and pare 2 large beets; grate coarsely (easy to do if you leave 3 or 4 inches of stems for handles). Chop onion, add with beets to boiling broth, and cook 15 to 20 minutes. Add drained beans and cabbage; cook 10 minutes. Don't overcook. Add butter, lemon juice, salt, and pepper. Serve with a spoonful of sour cream in each bowl.

Lentil Soup

Makes 6 servings

- 6 slices bacon, diced
- 2 onions, chopped
- 1 stalk celery, chopped
- 3 carrots, chopped
- 1 pound lentils, rinsed
- 2 cans (10½ ounces each) condensed beef broth, undiluted
- 1 bay leaf
  Salt and pepper to taste
- 4 cups water
  Sieved hard-cooked egg

Microwave: Combine bacon, onions, celery, and carrots in 4-quart casserole. Cover tightly with Saran Wrap, turning back edge to vent. Microcook at 100% power 8 minutes, stirring once. Add lentils, beef broth, bay leaf, salt, pepper, and 3 cups hot tap water. Recover, leaving vent, and microcook at 100% power 10 minutes. Stir well, recover, and microcook at 70% power 30 minutes, or until lentils are tender, stirring once or twice. Let stand 5 minutes. Remove bay leaf and serve garnished with sieved hard-cooked egg.

Conventional: Sauté bacon, onions, and celery in large saucepan until onions are transparent and bacon is crisp. Stir in carrots, lentils, beef broth, bay leaf, salt, pepper, and water. Heat to boiling. Reduce heat, cover and simmer 40 minutes, or until lentils are tender. Serve as above.

Chili Bean Soup

Makes 5 to 6 cups

- 1 pound pink, red, or pinto beans
- 6 to 8 cups boiling water
- 1 teaspoon garlic salt
- 1 teaspoon onion salt
- ¼ teaspoon *each* thyme and marjoram
- 1 can (10½ ounces) beef or chicken broth
- 1 can (16 ounces) stewed tomatoes
- 1 package (1⅝ ounces) chili seasoning mix or 1 can (7 to 10 ounces) green chile salsa
- 1 cup hot water

Rinse, sort, and soak beans. Drain and empty into a large pot. Add boiling water, garlic salt, and onion salt, thyme, and marjoram. Cover and simmer until beans are tender, 2½ to 3 hours. Don't let beans boil dry. Add hot water as needed. Spoon out 3 cups of the cooked beans to use another day in another way. Mash rest of beans with their liquid. Add remaining ingredients, plus 1 cup hot water. Heat at least 10 minutes to blend flavors.

Old-Fashioned Ham Bone Soup

Makes 6 to 8 servings

- 2 cups small white beans, soaked and drained
- 2 quarts cold water
- 1 meaty ham bone or 2 smoked ham hocks
- 6 peppercorns
- 1 small bay leaf
- 1 medium onion, chopped
  Parsley
  Green onions
  Croutons
  Grated cheese
  Paprika
  Hot water or chicken broth

To make it like Grandma did, about 4 hours before you plan to serve, cover soaked beans with water. Add the ham bone, peppercorns, and bay leaf. Bring to a boil, reduce heat, cover, and simmer 3 to 3½ hours until very tender. Add onion the last hour of cooking. When done, take out ham and bay leaf, mash beans lightly, cut meat from bones into bite-size pieces, and return to the soup. Serve with a garnish of parsley, green onion, croutons, grated cheese, or paprika. Thin with hot water or broth, if desired.

Kasha-Pea Soup

Makes 8 generous servings

- 1 pound split peas
- ½ cup uncooked coarse kasha
- 2 quarts water
- 1 carrot, diced
- 1 medium onion, chopped
- 1 beef neck bone or ham bone
  Salt and pepper
  Sour cream (optional)
  Paprika (optional)

In soup kettle or Dutch oven, combine all ingredients except salt, pepper, and sour cream. Bring to boiling; reduce heat, cover. Simmer 1½ to 2 hours, stirring occasionally. Add more water, if necessary. Remove bones and adjust seasoning. Serve hot with dollop of sour cream and dash of paprika, if desired.

Sopa de Calabaza

Makes 6 servings

      2 tablespoons butter or margarine
      1 cup chopped celery
    ½ cup chopped onion
      2 cans (10¾ ounces each) chicken broth
      1 can (16 ounces) Libby's Solid Pack Pumpkin
      2 tablespoons chopped green chilies
  1½ teaspoons ground cumin
      1 teaspoon salt
        Dash pepper
      2 eggs, lightly beaten
      1 cup half and half
      2 cups (8 ounces) shredded sharp cheddar cheese
        Coarsely chopped tomato
        Corn chips (optional)

In 3-quart saucepan, sauté celery and onion in butter. Add broth; bring to boil. Reduce heat to simmer. Add pumpkin, chilies, and seasonings. Stir with a wire whisk until well blended. Cover; simmer 10 minutes. Remove ½ cup pumpkin mixture; gradually add to eggs, stirring constantly. Gradually add egg mixture back into soup, stirring constantly. Cook over low heat 5 minutes. Add half and half and cheese; heat thoroughly. Do not boil. Garnish with coarsely chopped tomato; serve with corn chips, if desired.

Hearty Golden Soup

Makes 4 to 6 servings

    ½ cup chopped onion
    ½ cup chopped celery
      2 tablespoons butter or margarine
      2 cups chicken broth
      2 cups sliced mushrooms
    ½ cup uncooked rice
    ½ teaspoon salt
    ½ teaspoon tarragon
      1 can (16 ounces) Libby's Solid Pack Pumpkin
      2 cups half and half
    ¼ cup dry sherry

In medium saucepan, sauté onion and celery in butter. Add broth, mushrooms, rice, and seasonings. Bring to boil. Cover; simmer 20 minutes, or until rice is cooked. Stir in pumpkin; continue cooking 5 minutes. Stir in remaining ingredients; heat thoroughly.

How to Make a Bouquet Garni

This is a tied-together collection of flavoring agents for long-cooking dishes such as soups, stews, and casseroles. The point of tying these things together is that they can be neatly and easily taken out and discarded at the end of the cooking process.

The simplest bouquet garni consists of a few sprigs of parsley tied together to be used in a concoction where parsley flavor is wanted but bits of parsley throughout are not desirable. A somewhat more subtle, but still simple bouquet combines parsley, bay leaf, and thyme. All sort of herbs—tarragon, chervil, basil, savory, rosemary, marjoram, and many others—can be used, alone or in combination with vegetables such as chives, leeks, and celery. In fact, 2 stalks of celery or a split leek can serve as the outer casing of a bundle, with herbs tied securely within. Use ordinary white kitchen twine to hold the bundle together, tying in several places.

If dried herbs and/or other flavorings, such as garlic, orange or lemon peel, and peppercorns are used, the bouquet is usually placed in a square of cheesecloth, the ends gathered together and tied into a neat little bag so that the small bits of flavoring don't disperse themselves through the liquid. The bag is easy to remove when the dish is ready to be served.

Mulligatawny Soup

Makes 6 servings

      2 leeks, cut into julienne strips
      1 small onion, cut into thin strips
      1 small apple, cored, peeled, and finely diced
    ¼ cup butter
    ¼ teaspoon curry powder
    ¼ cup all-purpose flour
      2 cans (10½ ounces each) Campbell's Condensed
        Chicken Broth
      1 ripe tomato, chopped
      2 cups heavy cream
    ½ cup cooked rice
        Salt and pepper

Sauté leeks, onion, and apple in butter until pale golden brown. Stir in curry powder and flour. Slowly blend in chicken broth; add tomato; stir constantly until smooth and thickened. Simmer slowly 20 minutes. Stir in cream and rice. Reheat but do not boil. Season to taste with salt and pepper.

Meaty Main-Dish Soups

When you need a meal-in-a-dish—and most of these handsome soups can be prepared ahead!

Creamy Clam Chowder

Makes 4 servings

- 4 tablespoons butter or margarine, divided
- 1 small onion, finely chopped
- ¼ cup minced celery
- 2 tablespoons all-purpose flour
- 1 cup diced potatoes
- 2 cups chicken or clam broth, or a mixture
- 1 can minced clams, reserving liquid
- 1 cup heavy cream
- ½ cup dry white wine
- Salt and pepper to taste

Heat 2 tablespoons butter in large pot. Add onions and celery and saute until golden. Sprinkle the flour over the onion-celery mixture and cook 3 minutes, stirring constantly. Add potatoes and broth, including the reserved clam liquid. Cover and simmer about 10 minutes. Add clams and simmer 10 minutes more, until potatoes are tender. Stir in cream, wine, 2 tablespoons butter, salt, and pepper. Heat until the butter has melted. Serve immediately.

New England Clam Chowder

Makes 8 servings

- 2 cans Doxsee Minced Clams, reserve liquid
- ½ cup butter
- 1 large onion, chopped
- 2 large potatoes
- Salt and pepper to taste
- 2 cups milk or light cream
- Crisp crackers

Drain clams, reserving liquid. Heat butter in a saucepan. Cook onion until golden. Add potatoes and clam liquid. Cover and simmer slowly until potatoes are tender, about 15 minutes. Add minced clams and seasonings. Cook 3 minutes. Add milk. Heat but do not boil. Serve at once with crisp crackers.

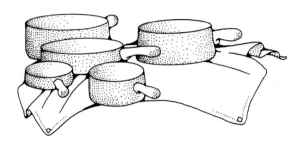

Mediterranean Fish Stew

Makes 4 servings

- 2 tablespoons margarine or butter
- ½ cup frozen small whole onions, thawed
- 1 clove garlic, finely chopped
- 1 can (16 ounces) stewed tomatoes, undrained
- 2 medium carrots, pared and sliced
- 1 tablespoon Wyler's® Chicken-Flavor Instant Bouillon or 3 Chicken-Flavor Bouillon Cubes
- ½ teaspoon marjoram leaves
- 1 bay leaf
- Dash pepper
- 1½ cups water
- 2 tablespoons all-purpose flour
- 1 pound fresh or frozen fish fillets (haddock, sole, or perch), thawed if frozen, cut into large chunks
- 1 jar (2½ ounces) sliced mushrooms, drained
- 1 small green pepper, seeded and cut into 1-inch pieces

In medium saucepan, cook onions and garlic in margarine 5 minutes. Add tomatoes, carrots, bouillon, marjoram, bay leaf, and pepper. Combine water and flour; mix well. Stir into tomato mixture. Cover and simmer 30 minutes, or until carrots are tender; remove bay leaf. Stir in fish, mushrooms, and green pepper. Cover; cook 5 minutes, or until fish flakes with fork. Serve immediately. Refrigerate leftovers.

Creamy Clam Chowder. Gordon E. Smith

Fisherman's Chowder

Makes about 8 servings

    3 tablespoons oil
    1 cup chopped onions
    ½ cup diced carrot
    ½ cup diced celery
    2 tablespoons all-purpose flour
    2 cups water
    1 can (1 pound) tomatoes, broken up
    2 packages (12 ounces each) frozen haddock
        fillets, thawed and cut into 1-inch pieces
    1 tablespoon Lea & Perrins Worcestershire Sauce
    1 teaspoon salt
    ¼ cup chopped parsley
      Oyster crackers (optional)

In a large saucepan, heat oil. Add onions, carrots, and celery; sauté until tender, about 5 minutes. Blend in flour; cook and stir for 2 minutes. Add water and tomatoes; bring to boiling point. Add fish, Lea & Perrins, and salt. Reduce heat and simmer covered 15 minutes longer. Stir in parsley. Serve with oyster crackers, if desired.

Tuna Chowder

Makes 6 to 8 servings

    1 medium onion, cut in eighths
    1 cup water
    2 tablespoons butter or margarine
    2 cans (7 ounces each) tuna, drained and flaked
   12 sprigs parsley
    1 cup milk
    2 cans (about 10 ounces each) condensed potato
        soup
    ¼ teaspoon pepper

Blender-chop onion with water. Drain, reserving liquid. Melt butter in saucepan and sauté until soft. Add flaked tuna and remove from heat. Put parsley, milk, reserved water, soup, and pepper into blender. Cover and process at Chop until parsley is chopped. Pour into saucepan; mix well with onions and tuna. Simmer over low heat about 15 minutes. If a thinner chowder is desired, an additional cup of water or milk may be added.

Fish Stock Substitute

Mix equal parts bottled clam juice with water mixed with a little dry white wine or Vermouth simmered a few minutes with chopped onion and several parsley sprigs.

Clam-Lima Chowder

Makes 6 to 8 servings

    3⅓ cups drained, cooked or canned white baby
        lima beans
    2 ounces salt pork
    ½ cup chopped onion
    2 tablespoons butter or margarine
    2 tablespoons all-purpose flour
    2 cans (6½ ounces each) minced clams
    1½ cups *each* milk and half and half
    ½ teaspoon Worchestershire sauce
      Cayenne pepper and salt
    ½ cup sliced green onion
      Oyster crackers

Purée the cooked beans with their cooking liquid, adding enough water to make 1 to 1½ cups. Cut salt pork into ½-inch cubes and fry until lightly browned. Remove salt pork and sauté chopped onion in the fat. Don't brown. Add butter; blend in flour. Drain clams; save the broth and add water to make 1 cup. Stir clams, broth, milk, half and half, Worcestershire sauce, and a dash of cayenne into onion mixture. Cook and stir until thickened. Add puréed beans and salt pork. Heat thoroughly but do not boil. Salt to taste and garnish with green onion. Serve in individual bowls with oyster crackers.

Variation

Substitute comparable amounts of chopped shrimp, oysters, cubed whitefish fillets, or flaked canned tuna for the clams.

Crab Soup with Marsala

Makes 4 to 6 servings

    2 medium onions, finely chopped
    1 package (6 ounces) frozen crab meat, thawed
        and drained thoroughly
    2 tablespoons butter
    1 cup Ragú Homestyle Spaghetti Sauce
    2 tablespoons chopped fresh dill
    1 tablespoon lemon juice
    1 tablespoon Marsala
    2 pints half and half
      Salt to taste
      Pepper to taste
      Thinly sliced scallions

In a large saucepan, sauté onions and crab meat in butter until onions are translucent. Add spaghetti sauce, dill, lemon juice, and Marsala; simmer over low heat until heated through. Add half and half, salt, and pepper; heat through. Sprinkle with scallions and serve.

Quarter-Hour Soup

Makes 6 to 8 servings

    4 tablespoons olive oil
    1 clove garlic, chopped
    ½ pound fresh shrimp, shelled, deveined, and
        diced
    1 can (10½ ounces) Campbell's Condensed
        French Onion Soup
    1 can (11 ounces) Campbell's Condensed Tomato
        Bisque Soup
    2 soup cans water
    ⅛ teaspoon crumbled saffron
    1 tablespoon minced parsley
    ½ pound chicken livers
    ¼ cup raw rice, cooked and drained
    1 hard-cooked egg, finely chopped
        White bread

Heat 2 tablespoons olive oil and sauté garlic until golden. Add shrimp and continue cooking until shrimp become pink and opaque. Add soups, water, saffron, and parsley. Stir and simmer for 5 minutes. Heat 2 tablespoons olive oil and sauté chicken livers until brown and well cooked, about 10 minutes. Cube livers; add livers, cooked rice, and egg to soup. Simmer 5 minutes. Serve with cubed white bread sautéed in olive oil until golden brown.

Fish-Potato Chowder

Makes 6 servings

    2 tablespoons butter or margarine
    1 cup chopped onions
    2 medium potatoes, washed and diced (2 cups)
    ½ cup thinly sliced celery
    ¼ cup dry white wine
    1 teaspoon salt
    ½ teaspoon dill weed
    ⅛ teaspoon pepper
    1 small bay leaf
    1 can (13 ounces) undiluted evaporated milk
    1 package (10 ounces) frozen haddock, cod,
        turbot, or similar fish, thawed and cut into
        1½-inch pieces

Melt butter in 3-quart saucepan. Sauté onions until transparent. Add potatoes, 2 cups water, celery, wine, salt, dill weed, pepper, and bay leaf. Cover and simmer 30 minutes, or until potatoes are tender. Stir in milk. Add fish. Heat to simmering; do not boil. Simmer until fish is opaque and flakes easily. Discard bay leaf.

Creamed Corn-Chicken Soup

Makes about 10 servings

    4 slices bacon
    ¼ cup chopped onion
    1 can (1 pound 1 ounce) cream-style corn
    1 can (10¾ ounces) condensed cream of chicken
        soup
    2 cups milk
    ½ cup water
    1 envelope (.19 ounces) chicken-flavored broth
        mix
    1 tablespoon Lea & Perrins Worcestershire Sauce
    ½ teaspoon salt
    ¼ cup chopped parsley

In a large saucepan, fry bacon until crisp; drain on paper towels; crumble and set aside. In drippings left in saucepan, sauté onion for 2 minutes. Stir in corn, soup, milk, water, chicken broth mix, Lea & Perrins, and salt. Bring to boiling point. Reduce heat and simmer uncovered 2 minutes longer. Stir in parsley and reserved bacon.

Chicken-Summer Vegetable Soup

Makes about 6 cups

    3 cups chicken broth
    2 cups water
    3 ounces (half a 6-ounce package) dehydrated
        Idaho® Hash Brown Potatoes with Mild
        Sweet Onion
    1 teaspoon salt
    ½ teaspoon dried basil, crumbled
    ¼ teaspoon dried thyme, crumbled
    1 small zucchini, sliced (about 1 cup)
    1 large tomato, cut in chunks
    2 cups shredded lettuce
    1 cup shredded cooked chicken

In large saucepot, combine broth, water, dehydrated potatoes, salt, basil, and thyme; cover; bring to boiling. Reduce heat, simmer 15 minutes. Add zucchini and tomato; mix well. Cook 10 minutes longer. Stir in lettuce and chicken. Heat through.

Mediterranean Fish Stew (page 39). Wyler's® Bouillon

Chicken Soup with Matzoh Balls

Makes 4 servings

- 1 3-pound chicken or 3 pounds chicken parts
- 2 stalks celery
- 1 onion, quartered
- 1 carrot
- 3 sprigs parsley
  Salt and pepper to taste
  Matzoh Balls (recipe follows)

Place chicken, celery, onion, carrot, parsley, salt, and pepper in heavy 2-quart soup pot. Cover with cold water. Bring water to a boil, then lower heat and simmer for 1 hour. While soup is cooking, skim off foam that forms on top several times. (To do this, gently move a spatula or wooden spoon over the surface.) Ten minutes before serving time, add matzoh balls. When cooking is complete, pour liquid through a sieve into serving bowl. Serve with Matzoh Balls.

Matzoh Balls

- 2 eggs
- 6 tablespoons matzoh meal
  Salt and pepper to taste
- 1 tablespoon chicken or other fat (optional)

Break eggs into small mixing bowl and beat until lemon colored. Beat in matzoh meal, 1 tablespoon at a time; mix until it forms a paste. Add salt and pepper, and fat, if desired. Refrigerate at least 30 minutes. Mix again before cooking; if the mixture is too stiff to handle, add a tablespoon of soup to it. Drop by rounded tablespoons into boiling soup; cook at least 10 minutes.

Chicken Soup with Matzoh Balls. Calabro Studios

Wonton Soup (page 44). Wyler's® Bouillon

Chicken Gumbo Soup

Makes 4 to 6 servings

    2 tablespoons bacon fat
    1 medium-size onion, diced
    ½ cup diced green pepper
    2 stalks celery, sliced
    1 quart chicken or turkey stock
    2 cups canned tomatoes
    1 teaspoon salt
    ⅛ teaspoon pepper
    ⅓ cup uncooked rice
    1 cup canned or cooked okra
    1 to 2 cups diced cooked chicken or turkey
    2 tablespoons chopped parsley

Set dial of Sunbeam Multi-Cooker Frypan at 300°F. Melt fat. Add onion, green pepper, and celery. Fry, stirring constantly, until partially tender, but do not brown. Add chicken stock, tomatoes, salt, pepper, rice, and okra. When mixture is boiling, turn dial to Simmer. Cover and simmer about 40 minutes. Add cooked chicken and heat. Serve with chopped parsley.

Cantonese Soup

Makes 6 servings

    ½ pound lean pork, sliced thin
    2 tablespoons cooking oil
    2 tablespoons La Choy Soy Sauce
    ¼ teaspoon pepper
    1 teaspoon ground ginger
    1½ quarts chicken broth
    3 cups thin-sliced Chinese cabbage
      La Choy Chow Mein Noodles

In saucepot, lightly brown pork in hot oil, stirring frequently. Stir in soy sauce and seasonings; cook for 5 minutes. Add broth; simmer 15 minutes. Add cabbage to soup. Cook until cabbage is tender, about 5 minutes. Sprinkle noodles over each serving.

Soup-Bone Soups

With a few bits of meat clinging to it, the bone of any meat, the carcass of any poultry should say "soup" to you. Simmer a lamb bone with bay leaf; add carrots and barley. A ham bone (or a tag end of bacon) flavors pea, bean, or lentil whole-meal soups. Slow-cook a beef bone, add celery, lima beans, and onion. Make broth with a chicken carcass, add snipped watercress leaves, cook little dumplings in it just before serving. Bone-based soups are all the better for being made the day before serving. Refrigerate, then take off the congealed fat that will have risen to the surface before reheating.

Wonton Soup

Makes about 1½ quarts

    4 quarts water
    20 Wontons (recipe follows)
    8 teaspoons Wyler's® Chicken-Flavor Instant
      Bouillon or 8 Chicken-Flavor Bouillon Cubes
    1 cup thinly sliced Chinese cabbage
    1 pound sliced fresh mushrooms (about 4 cups)
    1 package (6 ounces) frozen snow peas, thawed
      Chopped green onion

In a large saucepan, bring 2 quarts water to a boil. Drop 20 wontons, 1 at a time, into boiling water. Simmer uncovered about 3 minutes. Remove from heat and rinse with cold water. Drain. In same large saucepan, bring 2 quarts water to a boil; add bouillon, stirring until dissolved. Add remaining ingredients except green onion. Heat through. Serve garnished with green onion.

Wontons

Makes 40 wontons

    ½ pound ground pork
    1 can (4½ ounces) shrimp, well drained and
      finely chopped
    ½ cup finely choped onion
    ¼ cup finely chopped water chestnuts
    1 egg
    1 tablespoon soy sauce
    1 teaspoon grated ginger root or ¼ teaspoon
      ground ginger
    ½ teaspoon sugar
    ¼ teaspoon salt
    ⅛ teaspoon pepper
    10 egg roll skins, cut into quarters, or 40 wonton
      skins

In medium bowl, combine pork, shrimp, onion, water chestnuts, egg, soy sauce, ginger, sugar, salt, and pepper; mix well. Spoon 1 rounded teaspoon filling just off center of each wonton skin. Fold over at center. Gently press edges together and fold in half again lengthwise. Pull the 2 corners one over the other and press them together with a little water. A properly wrapped wonton resembles a nurse's cap. Use half the wontons for the soup. Wrap, label, and freeze remaining wontons for up to 1 month. Deep-fry thawed wontons and serve with a sweet and sour sauce, or use to make another batch of Wonton Soup.

Chicken Vegetable Soup

Makes 4 servings

  1 quart homemade or canned chicken broth
  ½ cup celery, diced
  ½ cup carrots, diced
  2 tablespoons onions, minced
  2 cups diced cooked chicken
  2 tablespoons snipped parsley

Heat broth to boiling in a heavy soup pot. Add celery, carrots, and onions. Simmer until vegetables are tender, at least 1 hour. Add chicken and parsley; simmer another 10 minutes and serve piping hot.

Oxtail Soup

Makes 8 servings

  2 pounds oxtails
  2 tablespoons cooking oil
  2 quarts water
  1 tablespoon salt
  ½ cup chopped onion
  1 cup sliced carrot
  ¾ cup sliced celery
  ½ cup sauerkraut, drained
  1 cup cooked tomatoes

Cut meat into 2-inch pieces. In skillet, brown oxtails in cooking oil. Remove to large kettle or Dutch oven and add 2 quarts of water and salt. Cover and simmer 3½ hours. Remove meat from bones and return meat to soup stock. Add vegetables. Cover and simmer 30 minutes. Skim off fat and serve.

Meatball Soup

Makes 6 servings

  ½ pound lean venison or lamb, ground twice
  ½ cup cooked rice, ground wheat, or bulgur
  ¼ cup finely chopped onion
  ¼ cup finely chopped parsley
  2 cans (10½ ounces each) Campbell's Condensed
     Chicken Broth
  2 soup cans water
  ⅓ cup lemon juice
  2 eggs
  Salt, pepper

Combine first four ingredients. Shape into ¾-inch balls. Heat broth and water to the simmering point. Add meatballs; simmer 15 to 20 minutes. In a soup tureen, beat lemon juice and eggs until smooth. Gradually beat in hot broth. Add meatballs last. Season to taste with salt and pepper.

Meatball Soup with Sherry

Makes 6 servings

  1 pound ground beef
  ¾ teaspoon salt
  ¾ teaspoon chili powder
  1 small onion, very finely minced
  1 cup dry bread crumbs
  ⅓ cup pine nuts
  1 egg, beaten
  ⅓ cup sherry, divided
  2 cans (10½ ounces each) beef bouillon or
     consommé
  2 soup cans water
  1 bay leaf

Mix first 7 ingredients and 1 teaspoon sherry. Shape mixture into tiny meatballs about 1 inch in diameter. Put bouillon, water, and bay leaf into Sunbeam Multi-Cooker Frypan. Set dial at 300°F. When mixture is boiling, drop in meatballs, a few at a time, so that boiling remains constant. Reduce heat, cover, and simmer until meatballs are tender, about 25 minutes. Just before serving, remove bay leaf and stir in remaining sherry.

Poi Thick Soup

Makes 4 servings

  1½ pounds potatoes or taro root
  1½ pounds top round (½-inch-thick slice)
  ½ pound mushrooms, sliced
  1½ tablespoons oil
  ¼ cup chopped scallions
  1 can (10½ ounces) Campbell's Condensed
     Chicken Broth
  ¾ cup water
  ¼ cup soy sauce
  Salt
  2 tablespoons cornstarch
  ¼ cup cold water

Scrub potatoes. Cover with water and boil until tender. Drain, peel, and cut into ¾-inch cubes. Pound round steak until paper-thin. Cut steak into strips ¾-inch wide and 3 inches long. Sauté beef and mushrooms in oil until beef is just cooked. Add scallions, chicken broth, water, and soy sauce. Cover and cook for 5 minutes. Fold in potatoes. Season to taste with salt. Mix cornstarch and water, and stir into meat mixture. Cook, stirring, until mixture bubbles and thickens.

Chicken Vegetable Soup (page 45). Gordon E. Smith

Meatball Soup (page 45). Campbell Soup Company

Philadelphia Pepper Pot Soup

Makes 12 servings

     4 tablespoons Planters® Peanut Oil
  2½ pounds veal shank, cracked
     2 quarts water
   ½ teaspoon black peppercorns
   ½ teaspoon crushed red pepper
   ½ teaspoon ground black pepper
   ¼ teaspoon thyme leaves
   ¼ teaspoon ground marjoram
   ¼ cup all-purpose flour
     1 cup chopped onion
     1 cup sliced celery
   ½ cup diced green pepper
   ½ cup sliced carrots
     1 tablespoon salt
     1 can (16 ounces) tomatoes, undrained
   ¼ cup elbow macaroni
     2 tablespoons minced parsley

In a large saucepan, heat 1 tablespoon Planters® Peanut Oil over medium-high heat; add veal and brown well. Add water, peppercorns, red pepper, black pepper, thyme, and marjoram. Bring to a boil. Reduce heat; cover and simmer 2 hours. Strain stock through several thicknesses of cheesecloth. Dice veal; set aside. Blend together remaining 3 tablespoons Planters® Peanut Oil and flour in a large saucepot or Dutch oven over medium heat. Add onion, celery, green pepper, carrots, and salt. Chop tomatoes; blend into vegetable mixture. Cook over medium heat, stirring constantly, until mixture comes to a boil. Stir in prepared stock and macaroni; return to a boil. Cook 20 minutes, stirring occasionally, until macaroni is tender. Mix in veal and parsley; heat thoroughly and serve.

Vienna Sausage-Corn Chowder

Makes 5 cups

   ¼ cup chopped onion
   ¼ cup butter or margarine
   ¼ cup all-purpose flour
     3 cups milk
     2 cans (5 ounces each) Armour Star Vienna
        Sausage in Beef Stock, drained and sliced
     1 can (17 ounces) cream-style corn
     1 tablespoon chopped parsley
     1 tablespoon chopped pimiento
     1 teaspoon salt
   ¼ teaspoon pepper

Cook onion in butter until tender; blend in flour. Add milk; cook, stirring constantly, until thickened. Add remaining ingredients; heat.

Mock Bird's Nest Soup

Makes 6 to 8 servings

     1 bundle long rice or 1 cup uncooked fine egg
        noodles
     2 cans (10½ ounces each) Campbell's Condensed
        Chicken Broth
  2½ cups water
     4 large mushrooms, chopped
     1 cup minced fresh lean pork
     1 cup finely chopped smoked ham
   ½ cup chopped water chestnuts
     2 egg whites, lightly beaten
     1 tablespoon chopped Chinese parsley or parsley

If long rice is used, cut into ¼-inch lengths and soak in hot water 30 minutes. Heat chicken broth, adding the water to the broth. Add mushrooms, pork, ham, and water chestnuts. Drain long rice and add to soup. Bring to a boil and simmer 10 minutes. (If using fine noodles, just add them as they are to soup and cook about 10 minutes until tender.) Stir egg whites into broth. Simmer 5 minutes. Garnish each serving with chopped parsley.

Hearty Ham and Bean Soup

Makes about 10 servings

     1 meaty smoked ham shank, about 2 pounds
  2½ quarts water
   ½ cup dried red kidney beans
   ½ cup dried white kidney beans
   ½ cup dried pinto beans
   ¼ cup chopped onion
     3 tablespoons Lea & Perrins Worcestershire Sauce
     1 bay leaf
     2 cups sliced carrots

In a large saucepot, combine ham, water, beans, onion, Lea & Perrins, and bay leaf. Bring to boiling point. Reduce heat and simmer covered until beans are almost tender, about 2 hours. Stir in carrots. Cover and simmer until beans and vegetables are tender, about 1 hour. Remove ham shank; cut off skin from bone; discard. Cut meat into chunks; return to saucepot. Remove bay leaf. Heat soup until hot.

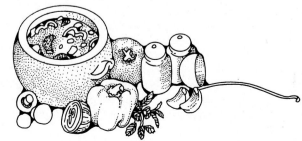

Creamy Delite-Split Pea Soup

Makes 8 servings
    1 pound dry split peas
    1 1½- to 2-pound Armour Star or 1877 Delite
    1 cup chopped onion
    2 tablespoons butter or margarine, melted
    1 tablespoon all-purpose flour
    1 tablespoon salt
    ¼ teaspoon pepper
    ¼ cup milk

Soak peas in water overnight. Drain; rinse. Cover again with water, add Delite and onion. Simmer 1 hour and 45 minutes, or until peas are tender. Remove Delite; cube. Drain peas, reserving liquid. Place peas and onion in blender; blend until smooth. Return to pan; combine with Delite cubes and 4 cups reserved liquid. Combine butter with flour, salt, and pepper; add to pea mixture. Bring to a boil; reduce heat. Stir in milk; simmer 30 minutes.

Make It Perfectly Clear

To clarify stock, place 2 quarts of cold, fat-free stock in a large saucepan. Beat 3 egg whites lightly and stir them into the stock. Add the egg shells—an essential part of the secret of clear stock. Heat the stock slowly to boiling, stirring constantly with a slotted spoon. When the mixture reaches a full boil, there will be a layer of sticky sediment on top. Set the pan aside, undisturbed, for 15 minutes. then pour the stock through a strainer lined with several thicknesses of cheesecloth wrung out in cold water. Let it drain for 15 minutes. Use the stock at once or refrigerate it, uncovered.

Sopa de Sonora

Makes 6 to 8 servings
    1 pound boneless lean pork shoulder, trimmed
        and cut into 1-inch cubes
    1 tablespoon salad oil
    1½ tablespoons Lawry's Minced Onion with Green
        Onion Flakes
    ¼ teaspoon Lawry's Garlic Powder with Parsley
    1 package (1⅝ ounces) Lawry's Chili Seasoning
        Mix
    4½ cups water
    1 can (14½ ounces) beef broth
    1 cup dried pinto beans, rinsed
    2 cups thinly sliced carrots
        Lawry's Seasoned Salt to taste
        Condiments: cherry tomatoes, cut in quarters,
        sliced green onion, chopped cilantro, lime
        wedges, sour cream, Lawry's Chunky Taco
        Sauce

In Dutch oven, brown pork in hot oil. Add remaining ingredients except carrots, Seasoned Salt, and condiments; blend well. Bring to a boil; reduce heat and simmer covered 1½ hours. Add carrots, cover and simmer covered about 30 minutes, or until carrots are tender. Add Seasoned Salt to taste. Serve with condiments.

Hungarian Goulash Soup

Makes about 2 quarts
    1 cup chopped onion
    2 cloves garlic, finely chopped
    2 tablespoons margarine or butter
    2 tablespoons paprika
    1 pound beef stew, cut into 1-inch pieces
    8 cups water
    1 can (16 ounces) tomatoes, undrained
    2 tablespoons Wyler's® Beef-Flavor Instant Bouil-
        lon or 6 Beef-Flavor Bouillon Cubes
    1 teaspoon sugar
    ½ teaspoon marjoram
    ⅛ teaspoon pepper
    1 cup pared diced potatoes
    1 cup chopped green pepper

In large saucepan or Dutch oven, cook onion and garlic in margarine until tender. Add paprika; stir until onions are coated. Stir in remaining ingredients except potatoes and green pepper. Bring to a boil; reduce heat and simmer uncovered 1 hour, or until beef is tender. Add potatoes and green pepper; cook 20 minutes, or until potatoes are tender. Refrigerate leftovers.

Corned Beef and Cabbage Soup

Makes 6 to 8 servings
    3 cups corned beef liquid, strained from cooked
        corned beef
    1 can (10½ ounces) beef broth
    1 can water
    1 cup cubed cooked corned beef
    1 cup shredded cabbage
    1 cup peeled diced potato
    ½ cup finely chopped onion
    ½ cup finely chopped celery
    ½ teaspoon Lawry's Garlic Salt
        French bread (optional)

In Dutch oven, place corned beef liquid, broth, and water; add remaining ingredients. Bring to a boil; reduce heat and simmer covered 20 minutes. Serve with warmed French bread.

Final Touches

Beautiful soup, that most versatile of dishes! A light soup gets a meal off to a great start. In the event of droppers-in at mealtime, a well-garnished bowl of soup can extend dinner for 4 to dinner for six without letting your panic show. Served with bread and salad, soup can be a meal in itself. Steaming mugs of soup serve as a pick-me-up after outdoor work or play in cold weather. Chilled soup can be a genuine refresher on a hot day, when appetites lag. And as a bonus, soup—both in the making and in the garnishing—can act as the ultimate medium for using up leftovers without anyone but you being the wiser.

Rafts and Other Beef-it-up Additions

It's traditional to garnish onion soup with a thick, lavishly cheesed slice of French bread, the whole thing run under the broiler for a few minutes before serving. Delicious and satisfying, right? What law says that the same idea can't be applied to almost any other soup-bread-topping combination?

Try rye bread with muenster on a vegetable soup that has cabbage as one of its ingredients. Top dark bread with crumbled blue cheese to lighten up a hearty beef broth. Cream cheese on white bread, sprinkled with snipped chives or parsley, finishes a chicken or delicate fish soup to perfection. Good, sharp cheddar on French bread goes well with pea soup; a bit of leftover ham tucked under the cheese turns the soup into a stick-to-your-ribs meal. Sourdough bread with a drift of Parmesan or Romano complements any hearty fish soup. Now that you've got the idea for composing rafts, try any combination that pleases you.

Will It Float?

Cream soups, clear soups, and purées cry out for something to break up their smooth, flat surfaces. Slices of hard-cooked eggs and a bit of chopped raw onion are traditional with lentil soup and are so good that there's no reason to break with tradition. Unsweetened whipped cream or sour cream or plain yogurt are delicious on cream of tomato soup; sprinkle the dairy topping with something—chopped parsley or watercress, paprika, chopped peanuts, chili powder, curry powder, turmeric, or fresh herbs—to relieve the whiteness and add zest. Give pea soup the same treatment. Or garnish pea or bean soup with a slice of fresh tomato sprinkled with basil.

Croutons are just what a smooth, creamy soup needs to give it crunch. You can buy them, plain or flavored, in packages, but you can also make them—cheaper and tastier, as almost all homemade things are.

Plain Croutons: Trim the crusts from day-old bread slices and cut the bread into cubes of any size that takes your fancy. Spread the cubes on a baking sheet and toast them in a 375°F. oven for about 15 minutes, or until they are crisp and brown.

Buttered Croutons: Butter the bread slices on both sides and proceed as you would to make plain croutons.

Flavored Croutons: Toss the cubes cut from 4 slices of bread in ⅓ cup French or Italian salad dressing; bake them as you would plain croutons.

Cheese Croutons: Use buttered cheese bread to make these. An alternate method is to sprinkle the top sides of buttered croutons with grated Parmesan or Romano cheese before baking.

Seasoned Croutons: Sprinkle buttered croutons with curry powder, chili powder, dried and crumbled basil, oregano, savory, marjoram, or thyme, or grated lemon, orange, or lime peel, or any combination of seasonings that strikes your fancy, before baking.

To add attractive substance to almost any soup, float whatever leftovers your refrigerator has to offer on top of the soup. Here are a few ideas to get you started: Frenched green beans, slivers of almost any kind of cheese, strips of ham or chicken, cooked pasta, chopped hard-cooked egg, bundles of quickly blanched vegetables such as carrots, turnips, broccoli stems, or a scattering of raw ones like scallions and mushrooms. Suit the garnish to the color (contrast with it) and the flavor (complement it) or the soup on hand. Raw vegetables, too, cut in shapes with small cookie or canapé cutters or in julienne strips, are fine soup garnishes. And don't make the mistake of downgrading our old friends parsley and lemon.

Festive Fruit Salads

Rainbow-bright, these are the jewels of the salad world.
Offer them as appetizers, side dishes—or even as dessert.

Lavish Layered Fruit

Makes 12 servings

1 each cantaloupe and honeydew melon
¼ watermelon
2 pints strawberries or 2 packages (10 ounces each) frozen strawberries, thawed
2 kiwis
1 pint blueberries or 1 package (10 ounces) frozen blueberries, thawed
½ pint raspberries (optional)
Fresh mint leaves
Very Berry Sauce (recipe follows)
Whipped cream (optional)

Cut melons in bite-size chunks or balls. Wash and dry berries, discarding any that are spoiled and reserving several for garnish. Slice strawberries; peel and slice kiwis. In a large bowl, place a layer of cantaloupe chunks on the bottom. Layer next with watermelon, honeydew, and strawberries. Repeat with more melons, if any remain, until you near the top of the bowl. Working from the outside edge, in concentric circles, overlap slices of strawberries, kiwis, blueberries, and raspberries, if desired, until you reach the center. Garnish with whole berries and mint leaves. Serve individual servings with Very Berry Sauce and a dollop of whipped cream, if desired.

Very Berry Sauce

1 package (10 ounces) frozen raspberries, thawed
Syrup of frozen blueberries or strawberries (optional)

Purée berries and syrup in a blender until thick and frothy. Pour through a fine sieve to extract seeds. Serve cold.

Lavish Layered Fruit with Very Berry Sauce. Calabro Studios

Gateway Salad

Makes 8 servings

⅔ cup salad oil
⅓ cup Heinz Wine Vinegar
3 tablespoons honey
2 teaspoons dry mint leaves
½ teaspoon salt
8 cups torn salad greens, chilled
1½ cups cantaloupe balls
2 fresh pears, sliced
1 avocado, peeled and sliced
1 cup grated sharp cheese

Combine first 5 ingredients in jar. Cover; shake vigorously. Chill to blend flavors. Shake again before tossing with salad greens and remaining ingredients.

Wintertime Fruit Salad

Makes about 6 servings

Large romaine lettuce leaves
3 bananas, cut into 1-inch slices
3 oranges, peeled and sectioned
2 grapefruits, peeled and sectioned
½ cup Wish-Bone® Chunky Blue Cheese or Sweet 'n Spicy French Dressing
½ cup salted peanuts (optional)

Line salad bowl with romaine lettuce leaves. Add banana slices, and orange and grapefruit sections; toss gently with Wish-Bone Chunky Blue Cheese Dressing and chill. Top with peanuts.

Pineapple Boats with Aloha Salad

Makes 8 servings

  2 cups California dried figs
  1 fresh pineapple
  1 cup mandarin oranges
  1 cup whipping cream
  2 tablespoons sugar
  ½ cup toasted flaked coconut
    Fresh mint (optional)

Slice dried figs. Slice pineapple in half; scoop out center; cut into bite-size chunks. Drain oranges. Arrange figs, pineapple chunks, and oranges in pineapple shells. Whip cream, stir in sugar and coconut (reserve some coconut for topping, if desired). Spoon over fruits. Garnish with fresh mint, if desired.

Apple-Spinach Salad

Makes 4 servings

  1 large red apple
  3 tablespoons cider vinegar
  ½ tablespoon salt
    Dash freshly ground pepper
  4 scallions, thinly sliced
  3 tablespoons butter or margarine
  3 tablespoons sesame seed
  ½ cup Sun-Maid® Seedless Raisins
  4 cups lightly packed fresh spinach
  2 hard-cooked eggs, chopped

Peel, quarter, core, and thinly slice the apple. Over a small bowl, cut each slice into thirds. Add the vinegar, salt, pepper, and scallions. Heat the butter in a small heavy skillet until it bubbles. Add the sesame seed and cook, stirring over medium-low heat, until the seeds are lightly browned. Stir in the raisins and cook 1 minute longer. Add raisin and butter mixture to the apple mixture. Stir until well combined and set aside. Rinse the spinach well in cool water and pat or spin dry. Stem the spinach and place the leaves in a large salad bowl. Add the apple mixture to the spinach and toss until well combined. Sprinkle with the chopped egg.

Fruity Salad Toss

Makes 4 to 6 servings

  1 small head lettuce, torn into bite-size pieces
  2 oranges, peeled and sectioned
  1 grapefruit, peeled and cut up
  1 apple, cut up
  ¼ cup Wish-Bone® Deluxe French Dressing

In a large bowl, combine all ingredients; toss.

Spinach-Orange Toss

Makes 8 servings

  ½ teaspoon grated orange peel
  ¼ cup orange juice
  ¼ cup oil
  2 tablespoons sugar or Featherweight Liquid Sweetening
  2 tablespoons wine vinegar
  1 tablespoon lemon juice
  ¼ teaspoon salt
  1 can (10½ ounces) Featherweight Mandarin Oranges, drained
  6 cups spinach or other greens, torn into bite-size pieces
  1 small cucumber, thinly sliced
  1 avocado, peeled and sliced (optional)
  2 tablespoons green onions, sliced

Combine orange peel, orange juice, oil, sugar, wine vinegar, lemon juice, and salt in a covered container and shake. Combine remaining ingredients in a bowl, add dressing, and toss lightly.

Tropical Waldorf Salad

Makes 6 servings

  2 medium-size red apples, unpeeled
  2 cups thinly sliced celery
  ¾ cup Sun-Maid® Seedless Raisins
  2 bananas, cut into ½-inch slices
  1 can (8 ounces) pineapple chunks, drained
  ½ cup toasted slivered almonds
    Chilled lettuce cups
    Coconut Dressing (recipe follows)

Prepare the Coconut Dressing. Quarter, core, and thinly slice the apples and combine with the celery, raisins, bananas, pineapple, and almonds. Fold in the dressing. Spoon the salad into lettuce cups and serve.

Coconut Dressing

  ½ cup mayonnaise
  ¼ cup shredded coconut
  1 tablespoon horseradish

Combine mayonnaise, coconut, and horseradish and mix well.

Tangy Waldorf Salad

Makes 6 servings
    3 cups diced unpared red apples (2 to 3 medium)
    1 cup sliced celery
    ½ cup sweet pickle relish, drained
    1 cup coarsely chopped walnuts
    3 tablespoons Sue Bee Honey
    3 tablespoons sour cream or mayonnaise
    ¼ teaspoon salt
    6 crisp lettuce cups

Lightly toss apples, celery, pickle relish, and nuts together. Blend Sue Bee Honey with sour cream and salt. Pour over apple mixture and lightly toss. Chill. Serve in lettuce cups.

Orange Sunshine Salad

Makes 4 servings
    ¼ cup salad oil
    Freshly grated peel of ½ lemon
    Juice of Sunkist® lemon
    1 tablespoon sugar
    1 tablespoon chopped parsley
    ½ teaspoon salt
    ¼ teaspoon dried dill weed or marjoram, crushed
    4 Sunkist® navel oranges
    1 small sweet onion

Combine salad oil, lemon peel, lemon juice, sugar, parsley, salt, and dill weed. Peel and slice oranges and onion. Add to dressing and chill.

Deluxe Pear Salad

Makes 4 to 8 servings
    1 cup (8 ounces) creamed cottage cheese
    ¼ cup thinly sliced celery
    ¼ cup coarsely chopped walnuts
    8 canned or fresh pear halves
    Lettuce leaves
    ¼ cup Wish-Bone® Deluxe French Dressing

In small bowl, combine cottage cheese, celery, and walnuts. Arrange pear halves on lettuce; fill with cheese mixture. Spoon Wish-Bone Deluxe French Dressing over pears.

Continental Avocado Salad

Makes 8 servings
    2 small hearts of celery
    2 small heads Boston lettuce
    1 avocado, peeled, pitted, and diced
    ¼ cup diced pimiento
    ½ cup French Dressing (see index)
    2 tablespoons blue cheese, crumbled (optional)

Cut celery into ¼-inch crosswise slices; place in salad bowl. Add lettuce, torn into pieces, avocado, and pimiento. Just before serving, pour on dressing and toss, or crumble 2 tablespoons blue cheese over salad before pouring on dressing, if desired.

Pear Cups with Fruit Salad

Makes 4 servings
    4 large pears
    3 tablespoons Wish-Bone® Russian Dressing
    1 tablespoon honey
    ¾ cup halved grapes
    1 banana, sliced
    ¼ cup shredded coconut

Cut thin slice lengthwise from side of pears and remove pulp, leaving ¼-inch shell to form cups. Reserve ½ cup chopped pulp. (Save remaining pear pulp to use in a fresh fruit salad.) In medium bowl, blend Wish-Bone Russian Dressing and honey. Add reserved ½ cup pulp, grapes, banana, and coconut; toss thoroughly. Spoon into pear cups; wrap and chill.

Fruit Salad Mix-ups

Almost any fruit mixture looks good and tastes good. Try a combination of honeydew, cantaloupe, and watermelon balls for a handsome color combination as well as a delightful assortment of close-but-different flavors. Or mix fresh pitted bing and Royal Ann cherries. Or fresh pineapple chunks and halved strawberries. Kiwis, grown now in the United States, make a beautiful (incredibly green, with tiny coal-black edible seeds) addition to any combination of fruits.

In the winter, grapefruit segments and slices of avocado taste as lovely as they look, or cheer up orange segments and banana slices with frozen raspberries, not quite thawed.

Some fruits go well in a tossed green salad—slices of avocado, sections of orange or grapefruit, chunks of apple or fresh pear, whole or halved (seeded) grapes, slices of fresh peach. Sometimes a vegetable-fruit alliance makes a nice change, as when you compose a salad of alternating slices of peeled oranges and paper-thin red sweet onions, or mix artichoke hearts with grapefruit segments.

Summertime Ambrosia

Makes 6 to 8 servings

- 6 **large nectarines or peaches, peeled and sliced**
- 3 **large Sunkist® oranges, peeled and sliced into half-cartwheels**
- 1 **large or 2 small bananas, peeled and sliced**
- 2 **tablespoons sugar**
- 2 **tablespoons fresh squeezed lemon juice**
- ½ **teaspoon almond flavoring**
- ½ **cup flaked coconut**

Combine fresh fruits with sugar, lemon juice, and almond flavoring. Chill 2 to 3 hours. Spoon into dessert dishes. Top with coconut.

Q. *I know that if you cover fruits with lemon juice they won't turn dark, but is there any other way to keep them from darkening? All that sour lemon juice turns me off.*
A. It isn't necessary to use all that much lemon juice. Dilute the juice of 1 lemon with 1 cup of water for a solution that will prevent darkening. Or use orange or lime, or grapefruit juice if you prefer one of those flavors. Hard fruit, such as apples, can be slipped into a bowl of lightly salted plain water as you cut them up. Or resort to one of the commercial browning inhibitors. They are largely ascorbic acid (vitamin C) and do the job well. Find them shelved near the pectin and other canning products in your market, and follow label directions.

Summertime Ambrosia. Courtesy of Sunkist Growers, Inc.

Wikiwiki Yumiyumi (page 55). Courtesy of Calavo

Melon Surprise

Makes 6 to 8 servings
- 1 small melon (honeydew or cantaloupe)
- 2 cups fresh raspberries or strawberries
- ½ cup pineapple chunks or peach slices
- ½ cup grapes
- 2 tablespoons Karo Light Corn Syrup
- 2 tablespoons cherry-flavored liqueur

From 1 end of melon, slice off piece to make 4- to 5-inch round opening. Remove seeds with spoon; then remove melon meat in bite-size pieces with fruit-ball cutter or spoon. In medium bowl, lightly toss together melon, raspberries, pineapple, grapes, corn syrup, and liqueur. Refill melon with fruit. Replace top and refrigerate 1 to 2 hours. Spoon fruit from melon to serve.

Orange Walnut Salad

Makes 8 servings
- 8 medium oranges, sectioned
- 1 large bunch watercress, stems removed
- 2 to 3 Belgian endives, leaves separated, or 1 small head of Boston lettuce
- 1 cup Colombo Original Plain Yogurt
- 1 tablespoon Dijon-style mustard
- 1 tablespoon orange juice
- 1 teaspoon salt
- ½ teaspoon white pepper
- 4 tablespoons chopped walnuts

Place endive leaves like petals of a flower around the edge of large salad plate or 8 individual plates. Top with watercress and orange sections. Mix last 6 ingredients and pour over salad centers just before serving.

Wikiwiki Yumiyumi

Makes 8 servings
- 1½ cups sliced mango
- 1 cup sliced banana
- 1 cup sliced grapefruit
- 1 cup sliced strawberries
- Juice of 1 Calavo fresh lime
- 2 tablespoons honey
- ¼ cup salad oil
- ⅛ teaspoon salt
- 6 lettuce leaves

Chill fruit. Blend lime juice and honey in small mixing bowl. Add salad oil and salt. Place chilled fruit (except strawberries) in large mixing bowl. Pour lime-honey mixture over fruit. Mix gently. Arrange fruit on lettuce leaves in individual salad bowls. Top with strawberries.

Orange Walnut Salad. Courtesy of Colombo, Inc.

Mandarin Salad

Makes 4 to 6 servings
- Sweet-Sour Dressing (recipe follows)
- ¼ cup sliced almonds
- 1 tablespoon plus 1 teaspoon sugar
- ¼ head lettuce, torn into bite-size pieces
- ¼ bunch romaine, torn into bite-size pieces
- ¼ cup Bac*Os imitation bacon
- 2 green onions, thinly sliced
- 2 medium stalks celery, chopped
- 1 can (11 ounces) mandarin orange sections, drained

Prepare Sweet-Sour Dressing. Cook almonds and sugar over low heat, stirring constantly, until sugar is melted and almonds are coated. Cool; break apart. Toss almonds, dressing, and the remaining ingredients in large salad bowl. Garnish with additional imitation bacon, if desired.

Sweet-Sour Dressing
- ¼ cup vegetable oil
- 2 tablespoons sugar
- 1 tablespoon snipped parsley
- 2 tablespoons vinegar
- ½ teaspoon salt
- Dash pepper
- 1 drop red pepper sauce

Mix all ingredients; refrigerate.

Fruit Salad Bowl

Makes 6 servings
  2 red apples, diced
  1 pear, diced
  1 banana, sliced
  1 cup diced celery
  ½ cup coarsely chopped walnuts
    Lettuce leaves
  ½ cup mayonnaise
  2 tablespoons lemon juice
1½ teaspoons sugar
1½ teaspoons Lea & Perrins Worcestershire Sauce

In a medium bowl, combine apples, pear, banana, celery, and walnuts; spoon into a lettuce-lined bowl. Combine remaining ingredients. Just before serving, pour dressing over salad; toss gently.

Fresh Fruit Salad with Poppy Seed Dressing

Makes about 4 servings
  ⅓ cup Mazola Corn Oil
  3 tablespoons white wine vinegar
  2 tablespoons honey
  1 teaspoon poppy seeds
  ½ teaspoon dry mustard
  ⅛ teaspoon salt
  5 cups assorted fresh fruits: blueberries, kiwi slices, melon balls or slices, pineapple slices or wedges, peach slices, or strawberry halves
    Lettuce leaves (optional)
    Melon wedges (optional)
    Cottage cheese (optional)

In 1-cup jar with tight-fitting lid, place corn oil, vinegar, honey, poppy seeds, dry mustard, and salt. Cover; shake well. Refrigerate. Shake thoroughly before serving. On lettuce-lined serving platter or on melon wedge arrange fruit. Serve with dressing. If desired, serve with ½ cup cottage cheese per serving.
Note: Use 2 tablespoons dressing per serving. Remaining dressing may be stored in tightly covered container in refrigerator.

Autumn Fruit Compote

Makes 3 servings
  8 California dried figs, halved
  1 can (1 pound) pears, drained
  1 can (10 ounces) mandarin oranges, drained
  ½ cup fresh grapes
  2 bananas, peeled and cut into chunks
  1 apple, cored and sliced
  3 tablespoons orange marmalade
  ¾ cup sauterne

Combine dried figs and fruits in large bowl. Mix marmalade with wine; pour over fruits and chill.

Wine Fruit Cup

Makes 6 servings
1½ cups dry white wine
  ½ cup sugar
  1 tablespoon lemon juice
1½ teaspoons anise seed
  ¼ teaspoon salt
  1 small stick cinnamon
  ½ cup Sun-Maid® Seedless Golden Raisins
  4 purple plums, sliced
  2 nectarines, sliced

In an enameled or stainless steel saucepan, combine the wine, sugar, lemon juice, anise seed, salt, and cinnamon stick and bring to a boil. Turn off heat and cool to room temperature. Combine the raisins, plums, and nectarines in a bowl and strain the cooled wine syrup over them. Cover and refrigerate for several hours, stirring occasionally.

Harvest Cider Salad

Makes 8 servings
  3 cups apple cider
  2 envelopes unflavored gelatin
  ¼ cup Sue Bee Honey
  1 can (6 ounces) frozen lemonade concentrate, thawed
  2 large red-skinned apples, cored and diced
  ¼ cup chopped celery
  ¼ cup chopped walnuts or pecans

Combine 1 cup of cider with gelatin in small saucepan. Let stand 5 minutes. Cook over very low heat until gelatin is dissolved, stirring constantly. Remove from heat and stir in Sue Bee Honey and remaining cider. Pour lemonade concentrate over diced apples and stir to coat all sides to prevent darkening. Remove apples and set aside. Stir lemonade into gelatin mixture. Refrigerate until mixture begins to get thick and syrupy. Stir in apples, celery, and nuts. Pour into 1½-quart mold and chill until firm.

Fruity Yogurt Dressing

Makes about 2 cups
  1 cup (16-ounce can) drained peach halves
  ½ cup undiluted Carnation Evaporated Milk
  ⅓ cup raspberry yogurt
  ½ teaspoon vanilla extract

Place all ingredients in blender container. Cover. Process until smooth. Cover and chill. Serve over fruit.

Up-to-Date Waldorf Salad

Makes 4 to 6 servings
- 1 envelope Knox₍ᵣ₎ Unflavored Gelatine
- ⅓ cup sugar
- 1½ cups boiling water
- ½ teaspoon salt
- ¼ cup lemon juice
- 2 cups unpeeled diced tart apple
- ½ cup chopped celery
- ¼ cup chopped pecans or walnuts
  Salad greens (optional)

In a medium bowl, mix Knox Unflavored Gelatine with sugar. Add boiling water and stir until gelatine is completely dissolved. Stir in salt and lemon juice. Chill, stirring occasionally, until mixture is the consistency of unbeaten egg whites. Fold in apple, celery, and pecans. Turn into a 4-cup mold; chill until firm. Unmold to serve. Garnish with salad greens, if desired.

Fruit Salad Dressings

Fruit salads need dressing. A half-and-half combination of mayonnaise and sour cream or whipped cream is very good. So is honey and lime juice in equal parts. Or make a fresh pineapple salad and sprinkle it liberally with grated cheddar cheese in lieu of dressing. Or find a recipe for old-fashioned boiled salad dressing and substitute orange juice for the vinegar it calls for.

Fold a drop or 2 of almond extract and a liberal sprinkling of nutmeg or slivered mint leaves and grated orange peel into sour cream to dress peaches, nectarines, or apricots. Thin whipped cream cheese with orange juice.

Nuts of almost any kind are an excellent addition to any fruit salad. So are slivered dates.

For children, combine bananas, white raisins, and pineapple, and dress with a mixture of three-fourths mayonnaise and one-fourth chunky peanut butter well blended.

Holiday Fruited Waldorf Salad Mold

Makes 10 servings
- 2 cans (30 ounces each) fruit cocktail in juice or extra light syrup
- 4 cups apples
- 2 cups celery
- ⅓ cup chopped parsley
- ⅔ cup chopped green onions
- ⅓ cup toasted slivered almonds
- 1 cup sour cream
- ¼ cup mayonnaise
- ½ teaspoon salt
- 1 teaspoon lemon juice
  Lettuce

Drain fruit cocktail well, reserving liquid for another use. In large bowl, combine fruit cocktail, apples, celery, parsley, green onions, and almonds. In separate bowl, mix together sour cream, mayonnaise, salt, and lemon juice. Toss dressing with fruit mixture. Turn into 10-cup mold and pack well. Chill several hours or overnight. Unmold onto lettuce-lined platter and serve.

Tangy Apricot Aspic

Makes 4 to 6 servings
- 1 envelope unflavored gelatin
- 1½ cups Heart's Delight Apricot Nectar
- 2 tablespoons sugar
- ¼ teaspoon salt
- ⅛ teaspoon prepared horseradish
- ¼ cup lemon juice
- 1 cup finely shredded cabbage
- 1 cup diced apple
  Salad greens
  Mayonnaise

Soften gelatin in nectar, sugar, salt, horseradish, and lemon juice. Heat gently, stirring until gelatin is dissolved. Chill until syrupy. Fold in cabbage and apple. Pour into mold; chill until firm. Serve on salad greens with mayonnaise.

Avocado Mold

Makes 6 to 8 servings
- ¼ cup lemon juice
- 2 envelopes unflavored gelatin
- 1 cup boiling water
- 3 ripe avocados, peeled, pitted, and cut up
- 1 cup sour cream
- ½ small onion, cut up
- 1 teaspoon salt
- ⅛ teaspoon pepper
  Salad greens

Put lemon juice in blender container. Sprinkle on gelatin; let stand 1 minute. Add boiling water. Cover; blend at low speed until gelatin is dissolved. Add remaining ingredients except salad greens to blender container in order listed. Cover; blend at high speed until smooth. Pour into 6-cup ring or other mold. Press plastic wrap against surface. Chill several hours, or until firm. Unmold onto salad greens just before serving.
Idea: If using a ring mold, fill the center with a seafood salad.

Frozen Mango Salad

Makes 12 servings

⅔ **cup evaporated milk**
4 **tablespoons lime juice**
½ **teaspoon salt**
1½ **tablespoons all-purpose flour**
1 **can (13½ ounces) pineapple tidbits (reserved syrup)**
1 **egg, lightly beaten**
2 **tablespoons vinegar**
3 **soft Calavo mangos, peeled, seeded, and sliced**
¾ **cup shredded coconut**

Chill evaporated milk in freezer until soft ice crystals form, about 45 minutes. When chilled, whip evaporated milk until stiff, about 1 minute. Add lime juice; whip for 1 additional minute, until very stiff. Meanwhile, combine salt, flour, reserved fruit syrup, egg, and vinegar in saucepan. Cook over medium heat, stirring constantly, until thickened; cool. Add mangos, pineapple, and coconut to cooled mixture. Fold whipped milk into fruit mixture and spoon into a 2-quart mold. Freeze until firm. To serve, allow to thaw slightly and invert onto serving plate. Slice.

Molded Lime and Blueberry Salad

Makes 8 servings

2 **boxes (3 ounces each) lime-flavored gelatin**
2 **cups hot water**
1¼ **cups cold water**
3 **tablespoons fresh lime juice**
 Mayonnaise or sour cream
¼ **teaspoon salt**
1½ **cups fresh blueberries**
 Salad greens

Dissolve gelatin in hot water. Stir in cold water, lime juice, and salt. First layer, pour small amount (½ inch) into bottom of 5-cup mold and add ¼ cup blueberries in mold and chill. Second layer, chill remaining gelatin slightly, then add 1¼ cup blueberries and pour into mold on top of first layer. Chill until firm. Unmold on greens and serve with mayonnaise.

Cherry Wine Mold

Makes 6 servings

1 **can (16 to 17 ounces) dark or light sweet cherries, pitted if necessary**
1 **package (3 ounces) cherry-flavor gelatin**
1 **cup boiling water**
½ **cup port or water**
⅓ **cup *each* sliced celery and chopped pecans**
 Lettuce
 Mayonnaise (optional)

Molded Lime and Blueberry Salad. Courtesy of Calavo

Drain cherries; reserve ¼ cup syrup. Dissolve gelatin in boiling water. Add wine and reserved syrup. Chill until partially set. Fold in cherries, celery, and pecans. Pour into 1-quart mold and chill until firm. Unmold onto lettuce-lined platter. Serve with mayonnaise.

Variation

Using fresh or frozen cherries, increase boiling water to 1¼ cups and omit syrup. Substitute 1½ cups pitted fresh or frozen sweet cherries for canned cherries.

Peach-Almond Soufflé Salad

Makes 4 to 6 servings

1 **cup hot water**
1 **package (3 ounces) orange-flavored gelatin**
½ **cup cold water**
2 **tablespoons lemon juice**
½ **cup mayonnaise**
¼ **teaspoon salt**
1½ **cups diced cling peaches, well drained**
1 **package (3 ounces) cream cheese, softened**
¼ **cup toasted slivered almonds**

Pour the hot water over gelatin in large bowl of Sunbeam Mixmaster Mixer. Stir until gelatin is dissolved. Add the cold water, lemon juice, mayonnaise, and salt. Beat at medium until well mixed. Pour into freezer tray. Chill in freezer or refrigerator until firm, about 20 to 25 minutes. Meanwhile, combine peaches, cream cheese, and almonds. Turn gelatin mixture back into chilled Mixer bowl. Beat at high speed until fluffy and thick. Fold in peach mixture. Pour into a 1-quart mold. Chill until firm. Unmold on chilled serving plate and garnish as desired.

Cranberry-Apple Waldorf

Makes about 8 servings

    3 envelopes Knox® Unflavored Gelatine
    ⅓ cup sugar
    1 cup boiling water
    3½ cups cranberry juice cocktail
    1 cup chopped apple
    ½ cup chopped celery
    ⅓ cup chopped walnuts

In large bowl, mix Knox Unflavored Gelatine and sugar; add boiling water and stir until gelatine is completely dissolved. Add cranberry juice; pour into 8- or 9-inch square pan and chill until mixture is consistency of unbeaten egg whites. Stir in apple, celery, and walnuts; chill until firm.

Sangría Fruit Salad

Makes 12 servings

    3 envelopes unflavored gelatin
    1 cup fresh orange juice
    ½ cup sugar
    ¼ cup fresh lemon juice
    2½ cups red wine
    1 bottle (7 ounces) club soda
    2 oranges, peeled and sliced crosswise
    1 banana, peeled and cut into 1-inch chunks
    2 peaches, peeled and sliced
    1 cup halved strawberries
      Fresh fruit, cut up

Sprinkle gelatin over orange juice in medium saucepan. Place over low heat; stir constantly until gelatin dissolves, 4 or 5 minutes. Remove from heat; add sugar and stir until dissolved. Add lemon juice, wine, and club soda. Chill, stirring occasionally, until mixture is consistency of unbeaten egg whites. Fold in fruit, turn into 8-cup mold, and chill until firm, several hours or overnight. Unmold and garnish with additional fresh fruit, if desired.

Cranberry Dream Salad

Makes 8 to 10 servings

    1 cup heavy cream
    1 cup crushed pineapple, drained
    1 can (1 pound) whole cranberry sauce, cut up
    2 tablespoons mayonnaise
    2 tablespoons sugar
    2 packages (3 ounces each) cream cheese,
      quartered
    ¾ cup walnuts
      Lettuce

Place cream in blender, cover, and process at Whip. Remove to large mixing bowl and add pineapple to cream. Put cranberry sauce into blender; cover and process at Mix until smooth. Add mayonnaise, sugar, and cream cheese and continue to process until well blended. Add nuts and process only until chopped. Fold into whipped cream and pineapple. Pour into tray and freeze. To serve, let stand at room temperature for 15 minutes and turn out on lettuce. Slice.

Cranberry Mold

Makes 6 servings

    ¼ cup water
    1 envelope unflavored gelatin
    1 package (3 ounces) cherry-flavored gelatin
    1 cup boiling water
    1 orange, seeded and peeled (white membrane
      removed)
      Rind of 1 orange
    1 can (1 pound) whole cranberry sauce
      Salad greens

Put ¼ cup water into blender. Add gelatin and the boiling water. Cover and process at Stir until dissolved. Remove feeder cap and add orange and rind. Process at Mince until rind is finely chopped. Remove cover and add cranberry sauce, processing only until blended. Pour into 1-quart mold. Chill until firm. Unmold onto bed of greens.

Dressed-up Fruit Salads

Any season of the year is fruit salad season. During cold weather, citrus fruit, melons, and other fruit brought from warmer climates taste like summer to winter-tired palates. And when the weather turns warm and the succession of local fruit begins, there's nothing quite as refreshing as a fruit salad. Such salads, nicely garnished, and with something pretty and substantial on the side, can be a delicious main dish when heat makes appetites favor light, cool-seeming food. Any time of the year a fruit combination can double as both salad and dessert. Good to taste, good to look at, versatile—what more could you ask?

Simple one- or two-fruit salads compose best on individual salad plates. Those made of several fruits, particularly for more than 3 or 4 people, compose beautifully on platters, trays, or large plates. Or fruits can take to the salad bowl, by themselves or combined with greens. The tender, more delicately flavored greens partner better with fruit than the strong- or bitter-flavored ones, both as bases for composed salads and in combination with fruit in a bowl of mixed salad.

Frozen Peach-Pecan Salad

Makes 8 servings

- 1 **cup heavy cream**
- 1 **cup mayonnaise**
- 2 **packages (3 ounces each) cream cheese, cubed**
- 1 **cup pecans**
- 8 **peach halves**

Place cream in blender. Cover and process at Whip; empty into large bowl. Put mayonnaise into blender; gradually add cheese cream, processing at Mix until smooth. Stop blender and add pecans; cover and process at Chop a few seconds. Fold the blended mixture into the whipped cream. Arrange the peach halves, hollow side up, in refrigerator tray. Pour the cheese and cream mixture over the peach halves. Cover tightly; freeze until firm.

Nectarine 'n' Cherry Gel Salad

Makes 8 servings

- 2 **envelopes unflavored gelatin**
- 1½ **cups fresh orange juice, divided**
- 1 **tablespoon sugar**
- 2 **containers (8 ounces each) plain yogurt**
- 3 **tablespoons honey**
- ½ **teaspoon vanilla extract**
- ¾ **teaspoon grated fresh lemon or orange rind**
- 1½ **cups diced peeled nectarines**
- 1½ **cups pitted halved cherries**
- ¼ **cup chopped walnuts or almonds**

In medium saucepan, sprinkle unflavored gelatin over 1 cup orange juice. Place over low heat; stir until gelatin dissolves, about 3 minutes. Remove from heat; stir in sugar, remaining ½ cup orange juice, yogurt, honey, vanilla, and lemon rind; stir until mixture is smooth. Chill, stirring occasionally, until mixture is consistency of unbeaten egg whites. Fold in nectarines, cherries, and nuts. Turn into a 2-quart bowl or 8 glass salad bowls and chill until set.

Summer Fruit Salad Rosé

Makes 6 servings

- 1 **envelope Knox® Unflavored Gelatine**
- 1 **cup water, divided**
- 1¼ **cups rosé wine**
- 1 **cup thinly sliced peaches**
- ½ **cup thinly sliced bananas**
- ½ **cup sliced strawberries**

In a medium saucepan, mix Knox Unflavored Gelatine with ½ cup water. Let stand 1 minute. Stir over medium heat until gelatine is completely dissolved, about 1 minute. Remove from heat. Add remaining ½ cup water and the wine. Chill, stirring occasionally, until mixture is the consistency of unbeaten egg whites. Fold in peaches, bananas, and strawberries. Turn into 6 individual dishes; chill until set.

Basic Salad Gel

Makes 4 servings

- 1 **envelope Knox® Unflavored Gelatine**
- 2 **tablespoons sugar**
- 1½ **cups juice, broth, or water, heated to boiling**
- 2 **tablespoons vinegar or lemon juice**

In a medium bowl, mix Knox Unflavored Gelatine with sugar. Add boiling liquid; stir until gelatine is completely dissolved. Stir in vinegar or lemon juice. Pour into a 2-cup bowl or individual dishes; chill until firm.

Molded Salad Gel: Decrease liquid by ¼ cup.

Crunchy Salad Gel: Prepare as for Molded Salad Gel, except chill mixture, stirring occasionally, until it is the consistency of unbeaten egg whites. Fold in 1½ cups cut-up vegetables, cooked meat or fish, or any combination of these. Turn into a 3-cup bowl, mold, or individual dishes; chill until firm.

Salad Molds with Pizzazz

Molds lend flair to party tables—a fish-shaped mold of salmon mousse, for example, can be the hit of the buffet both in looks and taste. Tall molds of shimmering gel are very handsome. For family meals, individual dishes or any size kitchen bowl can be used. Try unusual containers, too—tea cups, demitasse cups, brandy snifters, parfait glasses, or shells of fruit or vegetables, such as oranges, grapefruit, tomatoes, or green peppers.

Garnishes for Molded Salads

Use individual or assorted salad greens; watercress or parsley sprigs; nasturtium leaves; cucumber slices or fingers; tomato wedges; whole cherry tomatoes; carrot curls; lemon wedges; strips of pimiento; sliced olives. These are merely suggestions, to spark your own creativity. Let your imagination run riot. Almost anything pretty and edible can be used as a garnish.

For fruited dessert-salad molds, you might try a dollop of whipped cream or sour cream.

Good Health Vegetable Salads

For a change of pace, turn the vegetable course into the salad course—two for one. And what an irresistible way to make sure your family gets the vitamins they need.

Liberty City Salad

Makes 8 servings (about 8 cups)
- ⅔ cup salad oil
- ⅓ cup Heinz Wine Vinegar
- 1 tablespoon chopped parsley
- 1 teaspoon thyme, crushed
- ¼ teaspoon basil
- ¼ teaspoon rosemary
- ¼ teaspoon oregano
- ½ teaspoon salt
- ⅛ teaspoon pepper
- 6 cups torn salad greens, chilled
- 1 cup sliced fresh mushrooms
- ½ cup salami, cut in julienne strips
- ½ cup Provolone cheese, cut in julienne strips
- ½ cup diagonally sliced celery
- ½ cup onion rings
  Anchovies (optional)

Combine first 9 ingredients in jar. Cover; shake vigorously. Chill to blend flavors. Shake again before tossing with salad greens and remaining ingredients. Garnish with anchovies, if desired.

Spinach Salad Bowl

Makes 6 to 8 servings
- 2 quarts fresh spinach, torn into pieces
- ½ pound fresh mushrooms, sliced
- 2 hard-cooked eggs, sliced
- 4 slices bacon, crisp-cooked and crumbled
- ½ cup Wish-Bone® Italian or Robusto Italian Dressing

In a salad bowl, arrange spinach, mushrooms, eggs, and bacon. Just before serving, toss with Wish-Bone Italian Dressing.

Caesar Salad

Makes 4 servings
- 1½ quarts torn salad greens
- ½ cup croutons
- 2 tablespoons Hormel Bacon Bits
- 1 tablespoon grated Parmesan cheese
- 3 tablespoons cooking oil
- 1 tablespoon lemon juice
- ½ teaspoon Worcestershire sauce
- ¼ teaspoon garlic salt
  Dash pepper
- 1 egg

Combine greens, croutons, bacon, and cheese in salad bowl. Combine oil, lemon juice, Worcestershire sauce, garlic salt, and pepper until well blended. Break egg over salad; pour dressing over all. Toss gently but well until all ingredients are coated with dressing.

Cauliflower Tossed Salad

Makes 4 servings
- 1 quart mixed salad greens, rinsed and torn into bite-size pieces
- 1 cup small fresh cauliflowerets
- 1 small cucumber, sliced (about ¾ cup)
- 1 large tomato, cut into wedges
- 6 slices Borden® Lite-line® Pasteurized Process Cheese Product, cut into strips
- ¼ cup bottled low-calorie spicy-sweet French-style dressing

In large salad bowl, toss greens, cauliflowerets, cucumber, and tomato. Arrange cheese product over and among greens. Serve with dressing.

Great Greens (page 65). Calabro Studios

Zucchini Tossed Salad

Makes 6 servings
- 2 cups thinly sliced unpared zucchini or yellow squash
- 2 medium ripe tomatoes, cored and thinly sliced
- 1 small red onion, sliced
- ½ lemon, thinly sliced and seeded
- ½ cup olive or salad oil
- 2 tablespoons vinegar
- 2 tablespoons fresh lemon juice
- ¾ teaspoon salt
- ⅛ teaspoon pepper
- 1 clove garlic, minced (optional)
- 2 cups salad greens, torn into bite-size pieces

In a large bowl, mix zucchini, tomatoes, red onion, and lemon slices. Mix oil, vinegar, lemon juice, salt, pepper, and garlic in a small bowl; pour over vegetables. Cover and refrigerate several hours. At serving time, place greens in a salad bowl, spoon marinated vegetables on top, toss to mix well.

Savory Vegetable Salad

Makes about 8 servings
- 2 quarts mixed salad greens
- 1 package (10 ounces) frozen cut asparagus, cooked, drained, and chilled
- 1 can (4 ounces) button or sliced mushrooms, drained
- ¼ cup sliced radishes
- ½ cup Wish-Bone® Italian Dressing

In large bowl, arrange salad greens, asparagus, mushrooms, and radishes. Pour Wish-Bone Italian Dressing over salad; toss gently.

Fall Festival Tossed Salad

Makes 6 to 8 servings
- 2 quarts mixed salad greens, rinsed and torn into bite-size pieces
- 3 cups uncooked broccoli flowerets
- 3 cups uncooked cauliflowerets
- 2 cups sliced zucchini
- ¼ pound fresh mushrooms, sliced
- 1 cup (8 ounces) Wish-Bone® Italian Dressing
- ⅓ cup crumbled crisp-cooked bacon

In large salad bowl, combine salad greens, broccoli flowerets, cauliflowerets, zucchini, and mushrooms; chill. Just before serving, toss with Wish-Bone Italian Dressing and bacon.

Country Salad with Pompion Dressing

Makes 4 to 6 servings
- ½ head iceberg lettuce
- ½ cup chopped green pepper
- ½ cup radish slices
- ⅓ cup chopped carrot
- ⅓ cup chopped onion
- 1 large tomato, chopped
- 2 stalks celery, chopped
- 4 slices bacon, crisply cooked and crumbled
  Pompion Dressing (recipe follows)

In large bowl, tear lettuce into bite-size pieces. Add remaining ingredients. Toss with ½ cup Pompion Dressing. Serve immediately.

Pompion Dressing

Makes 2 cups
- ¾ cup Libby's Solid Pack Pumpkin
- ½ cup oil
- ⅓ cup lemon juice
- ¼ cup honey
- 3 tablespoons cider vinegar
- 1 tablespoon paprika
- 2 teaspoons Worcestershire sauce
- 2 teaspoons grated onion
- 2 teaspoons prepared mustard
- 1½ teaspoons salt
- ½ teaspoon celery seed
  Dash garlic powder

Combine ingredients in blender container. Cover; blend at medium-high speed 3 minutes, or until well-blended. Cover; refrigerate until ready to use.

Pittsburgh Tossed Salad

Makes 8 servings
- ⅔ cup salad oil
- ⅓ cup Heinz Wine Vinegar
- 1 teaspoon sugar
- 1 teaspoon grated lemon peel
- ½ teaspoon salt
- ¼ teaspoon thyme
- ½ pound fresh mushrooms, sliced
- 8 cups torn salad greens, chilled
- ¼ cup sliced green onions

Combine first 6 ingredients in large jar. Cover; shake vigorously. Chill to blend flavors. Add mushrooms to dressing 1 to 2 hours before tossing with salad greens and onions.

Great Greens and Their Complements

If you tear up a head of iceberg lettuce, dash on a little oil and vinegar, and call it "salad," you're missing one of the table's greatest pleasures. When it comes to making salad, it pays to be open-minded. Just about anything goes, and the greater the variety, the better the salad looks and tastes. Begin with a selection of greens and move on from there, adding flavor and texture—yes, and beauty—as you go. Here are some greens and non-greens to get you started.

Iceberg lettuce—Don't use it all the time, but don't forget it, either. Sturdy, it tears well, shreds well, and has mild flavor that complements stronger greens.

Bibb lettuce—Sometimes called limestone because of the soil in which it's grown. Small, exquisitely tender heads of deep green, with gentle flavor.

Boston lettuce—Related to Bibb in color and flavor, the heads are bigger with loose leaves shading from dark outside to pale yellow-green within. Mild, buttery flavor.

Leaf lettuce—Big, raggedy heads of loose leaves with ruffled edges, entirely deep green or, in some varieties, edged with a couple of inches of dark red at the top. If you have a garden, grow your own.

Romaine lettuce—Elegant, long, crisp, somewhat boat-shaped leaves. Tear into tossed salads, use as a "holder" for meat, fish, poultry or mixed-vegetable salads.

Escarole—Resembles a shorter-leaf, curly-edge romaine, and has a stronger flavor.

Chicory—Dark green leaves with frilly edges. Very strong flavor, with bitter overtones. Use sparingly for pep-up flavor.

Cabbage—The many kinds are new green cabbage, winter cabbage, Chinese cabbage (also called Napa), red (which is actually a lovely purple-red), savoy (with wrinkled, heavily veined leaves) and celery cabbage. Chinese and celery are the mildest in flavor. All occur in heads, and should be finely or coarsely shredded, depending on how you use them.

Watercress—Pungent, peppery, dark-green leaves; discard heavy stems.

Parsley—Ruffled-leaf (the familiar kind) and Chinese, also called cilantro or flat-leaf, Mexican, or Italian parsley. The latter is neither stronger nor more delicate than ruffled-leaf, but it is quite different in flavor. Try it.

Belgian endive—Small, pale-green-to-white heads, strong-to-bitter flavor. Use whole leaves in salad, or slice through the entire head crosswise into rounds.

Spinach—Young and tender leaves are used for salads, either in combination with other greens or alone with a hot bacon-onion-egg dressing. Discard stems.

Other greens—Try very young dandelion greens, from your lawn or from the produce department; strong, delightful flavor. Try young and tender nasturtium leaves from your garden—and the flowers, too, if you're feeling adventurous. Try herbs; young fresh basil with tomatoes, for example.

And some non-greens—All sorts of delicious things can be added to make a good salad better. Onions—sliced scallions, or Bermudas, or Spanish, or red onions. Uncooked mushrooms, thin-sliced. Cucumbers, sliced or chunked. Thin slices of cauliflower. Tomatoes, big ones sliced; cherry tomatoes left whole or halved. (But don't toss them with the salad. Add just before serving, or their juice will dilute the dressing.) Celery, cut in paper-thin slices. Tiny, young broccoli flowers. Jícama, the Mexican tuber that's so crisp. Radishes, sliced if large, halved if tiny. Carrots, coarsely shredded. Zucchini, sliced or shredded. And some of the vegetables we sometimes forget *are* vegetables—thin slices of pickle, drained capers, cool green avocados, slivered and toasted nuts, daikon, the mild white Japanese radishes, olives in the green or ripe stage, thin-sliced. And don't forget the garlic!

chicory

boston

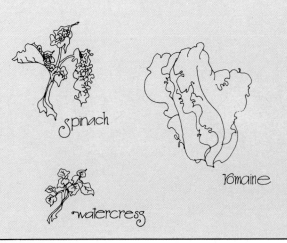

spinach

watercress

romaine

Greek Spring Salad

Makes 6 to 8 servings

      Sesame Seed Dressing (recipe follows)
6 **cups lightly packed fresh spinach**
½ **cup crumbled feta cheese**
½ **cup Sun-Maid® Seedless Raisins**
⅓ **cup pitted medium-size ripe olives**
¼ **cup thinly sliced radishes**
1 **hard-cooked egg, grated**
4 **scallions**

Prepare dressing. Rinse spinach in several changes of cold water. Pat or spin dry thoroughly. Tear the larger leaves into bite-size pieces, discarding the stems, and place in a salad bowl. Add the feta cheese, raisins, olives, and radishes. Toss well with the dressing and garnish with grated egg and scallions.

Sesame Seed Dressing

Makes ½ cup

¼ **cup olive oil**
2 **tablespoons lemon juice**
1 **teaspoon sesame seed**
1 **clove garlic, crushed**
1 **teaspoon oregano**
¼ **teaspoon salt**
⅛ **teaspoon freshly ground pepper**

Combine all ingredients in a small bowl or a jar with a tight lid. Beat briskly with fork or wire whisk, or shake until thoroughly mixed.

Greek Spring Salad with Sesame Seed Dressing. Sun-Maid Growers of California

Tomatoes with Avocado Dressing (page 67). Courtesy of Calavo

Caesar Salad (page 63)

Tomatoes with Avocado Dressing

Makes 4 servings
- 1 ripe Calavo avocado
- ⅓ cup mayonnaise
- 1 tablespoon lemon or lime juice
- 1 tablespoon onion juice
  - Dash Worcestershire sauce
  - Salt to taste
- 3 large tomatoes
  - Lettuce leaves
  - Chopped chives

Put avocado in blender or food processor. Mix with mayonnaise, add lemon juice, onion juice, Worcestershire, and salt. Peel 3 large tomatoes, slice and arrange on lettuce leaves. Pour dressing over tomatoes and sprinkle with chopped chives.

Marinated Tomato Salad

Makes 4 servings
- 1 pound (about 3 medium) tomatoes, sliced
- ¼ pound part-skim milk mozzarella cheese, thinly sliced (optional)
- ⅓ cup Mazola Corn Oil
- 3 tablespoons red wine vinegar
- 3 tablespoons chopped parsley
- 3 tablespoons finely chopped onion
- 1 tablespoon finely chopped basil leaves or ½ teaspoon dried basil leaves
- ¼ teaspoon salt
- ⅟₁₆ teaspoon pepper

Arrange tomatoes and cheese in bottom of shallow dish. In small jar with tight-fitting lid, place corn oil, vinegar, parsley, onion, basil, salt, and pepper. Cover; shake well. Pour over tomatoes and cheese. Cover; refrigerate several hours, spooning herb mixture over tomatoes occasionally.

Escarole Salad

Makes 4 servings
- ¾ cup Mazola Corn Oil
- ¼ cup red wine vinegar
- 1 teaspoon dry mustard
- ½ teaspoon salt
- ½ teaspoon dried tarragon
- ¼ teaspoon pepper
- 1 clove garlic, split
- 6 cups torn escarole leaves
- 1 cup red kidney beans, drained
- 1 cup zucchini strips (1½x¼ inches)
- ¼ cup sliced red onion

In 1-pint jar with tight-fitting lid, place corn oil, vinegar, mustard, salt, tarragon, pepper, and garlic. Cover; shake well. Refrigerate several hours. Remove garlic. In large bowl, toss together escarole, beans, zucchini, and onion. Serve with the dressing.

Chinese Vegetable Salad

Makes 6 servings
- ½ cup salad oil
- 2 tablespoons vinegar
- ½ teaspoon dry mustard
- ¼ teaspoon paprika
- 1 tablespoon sugar
- 1 teaspoon salt
  - Freshly ground pepper
- 1 clove garlic, crushed
- 3 cups finely sliced Chinese cabbage
- ½ cup thinly sliced carrots
- ½ cup sliced green onions
- 1 cup rinsed, drained La Choy Bean Sprouts
- ½ cup slices La Choy Water Chestnuts

Combine oil, vinegar, seasonings, and garlic; mix well. Chill for at least 1 hour. In a salad bowl, combine remaining ingredients. Pour salad dressing over vegetables. Toss lightly until vegetables are coated with salad dressing. Serve immediately.

Calico Bean Salad

Makes 8 to 10 servings
2 cups cooked navy, great northern, or small
    white beans
2 cups cooked or canned dark or light red kidney
    beans
2 cups canned or cooked garbanzo beans
1½ to 2 cups French, Italian, or vinaigrette dressing
    (bottled or homemade)
    Salt and coarse black pepper
    Vinegar (optional)
    Tomato wedges and onion rings
    Onion rings

Drain beans, mix together lightly, cover with dressing. Refrigerate for several hours. When ready to serve, mix again. Taste and add seasonings and a little vinegar, if needed. Serve in a large bowl and garnish with tomato wedges and onion rings.

Salad-Bowl Specials

Arugula is peppery green. Best when young and tender, so look for small, narrow, tender leaves and combine in a tossed salad with milder greens. Also called rocket (the English translation of its Latin botanical name), rocket salad, rocket cress, rucola, ruca and roka. *Limestone lettuce* is a soft-leaf mild, buttery lettuce, more delicately flavorful than its cousins, Boston and Bibb lettuce. *Mache* is mild-flavored, with a lingering taste that some compare to that of hazelnuts; it is also called corn salad (sometimes grown between rows of corn), field salad, or, most engagingly, lamb's lettuce. For a special treat (this is still one of the very expensive ones) make an all-màche salad dressed with a light vinaigrette and sprinkled with a little blue cheese. *Radicchio* has tender purplish leaves with white stalks and veins, and has a sharp, pungent flavor, far sharper than its red cabbage look-alike. A form of wild chicory, radicchio is part of the sunflower family. *Tamarillo,* a wonderful orange-to-scarlet color and shaped like an egg, is also known as the tree tomato because it grows on a shrub that can attain tree height, up to 15 feet. The flavor is sharp, slightly pungent, fine for use in mixed salads—both vegetable and fruit—or simply sliced; plain yogurt with a little honey and a sprinkling of mace makes a fine dressing for the tamarillo.

Mediterranean Salad

Makes 5 to 6 servings
1 pound dry baby lima beans
2 cups thin-sliced zucchini
2 tablespoons sliced green onion
1 can (2¼ ounces) sliced ripe olives
1 tablespoon chopped pimiento
2 ounces feta cheese, crumbled
    Caesar dressing (bottled or homemade)
    Leaf lettuce

Soak and cook beans according to package directions. (This will produce 5 to 6 cups cooked beans.) Divide into equal parts, using half for the salad; refrigerate the other half in a covered glass jar for use a day or 2 later. Combine cooked beans, zucchini, onion, olives, pimiento, cheese, and Caesar dressing and mix gently. Refrigerate covered until chilled. Serve on lettuce.

Hudson River Valley Hot Three-Bean Salad

Makes 6 servings
½ pound fresh green beans
½ pound fresh wax beans
½ cup sliced onion
1 cup water
1 teaspoon salt
2 tablespoons margarine
1 tablespoon Argo or Kingsford's Corn Starch
1 tablespoon brown sugar
¼ cup cider vinegar
1 can (15¼ ounces) red kidney beans, drained

Cut beans in 1½-inch pieces. In saucepan, bring first 5 ingredients to a boil. Cover; cook 8 minutes, or until tender-crisp. Drain and reserve liquid, adding water if necessary to make ¾ cup. In skillet melt margarine over low heat; stir in cornstarch until smooth. Remove from heat. Gradually stir in the ¾ cup liquid until smooth; add brown sugar. Bring to boil over medium heat, stirring constantly, and boil 1 minute. Stir in vinegar, cooked vegetables, and kidney beans. Reheat.

Bean Salad Tricks

Keep a jar of your favorite marinated beans in the refrigerator and

    1. Spoon them over wedges of iceberg lettuce, tomato slices, or mounds of cottage cheese.

    2. Serve in bowls or on relish trays with corn chips or crackers.

    3. Add color and flavor variety with diced green beans, red apple, or sliced dill pickles.

Bean Sprout Salad

Makes 2 servings

  2 ribs celery, finely chopped
  ½ cup chopped walnuts
1½ cups mung bean or soybean sprouts
  ½ teaspoon caraway seed
  2 Boston lettuce cups
  3 tablespoons Sue Bee Honey
  3 tablespoons lemon juice

Combine celery, nuts, sprouts, and seeds. Spoon into lettuce cups. Mix Sue Bee Honey and lemon juice together and dress salad to taste.

Bean Sprout Almond Salad

Makes 6 servings

  2 cups fresh or canned bean sprouts, rinsed and drained
  ½ cup sliced celery
  ½ cup toasted sliced natural almonds
  2 tablespoons *each* chopped green pepper and sliced green onions
  ¼ cup mayonnaise
  1 tablespoon lime or lemon juice
  1 teaspoon sugar
  ½ teaspoon paprika
  ⅛ teaspoon ground ginger
    Lettuce
    Paprika (optional)

In large bowl, combine all ingredients except lettuce. Toss to mix thoroughly. Line serving platter with lettuce leaves; top with bean sprout mixture. Dust with additional paprika, if desired.

Perky Picnic Bean Salad

Makes 4 to 6 servings

  1 can (16 ounces) pork and beans in tomato sauce
  1 cup sliced celery
  1 cup coarsely chopped green pepper
  1 tablespoon molasses
    Wish-Bone® Italian Dressing

In large bowl, combine all ingredients except Wish-Bone Italian Dressing. Toss with ¼ to ½ cup dressing, depending on consistency desired; chill.

Tossed-Salad Tip

Instead of cutting them, tear greens into bite-size pieces when preparing salad bowls—they will be more attractive and less likely to wilt or discolor. Mix several greens in salads to achieve contrasts in texture and color.

Black-eye Salad

Makes 8 servings

  1 pound (2 cups) Savory dry black-eyes (recipe follows)
  2 jars (4 ounces each) marinated artichoke hearts
  1 cup sliced raw radishes and/or carrots
  1 cup thinly sliced celery
  ½ cup sliced green onions
    French or Italian Drssing
    Pepper
    Lettuce leaves

Put beans in bowl and drizzle artichoke marinade over them. Cut hearts to bite size and add to beans with radishes, carrots, celery, and onion. Add your favorite French or Italian dressing to cover; add pepper to taste. Chill. To serve, spoon onto lettuce leaves.

Savory Black-eyes

  4 to 5 cups black-eyes, soaked
  6 cups hot water
  2 tablespoons shortening
  2 tablespoons onion salt
  ¼ teaspoon garlic salt
  1 tablespoon chicken stock base
  ¼ teaspoon white pepper

Drain and rinse soaked black-eyes; add water, shortening, onion salt, and garlic salt, chicken stock base, and white pepper. Simmer gently until barely tender. Drain while hot; cool beans quickly, uncovered.

Salad-Bowl Basics

No matter what anybody says, wash your salad bowl! It's true, some very prestigious cooking experts advocate using a wooden salad bowl and never washing it, simply wiping it out with absorbent paper after use. Stop and think a minute. Old oil gets rancid. And the smell and flavor of rancid oil are disgusting. Would you wipe off the dishes with a paper towel after dinner and consider them ready for the next meal?

A wooden salad bowl, attractive as it may be, is a very poor choice. If the inside of the bowl has a finish, mandatory washing will wear the finish away. If it is not finished, oil, vinegar, onion, garlic, anchovies, and all the other high smells/flavors of salad ingredients will sink into the wood and become impossible to remove. Handsome glass and ceramic bowls are available in a wide variety of shapes and sizes, and are a far more sensible—and hygienic—choice. Don't decide on a metal one, though. It will wash well, but it will give a metallic flavor to the salad.

Marinated Monterey Salad. Del Monte Corporation

Marinated Monterey Salad

Makes 6 servings

    Vinaigrette Dressing (recipe follows)
  4 medium red potatoes
  **1 can (16 ounces) Del Monte® Cut Green Beans
     (No Salt Added), drained**
  ½ head iceberg lettuce
  ½ cup chopped red onion
  **1 can (6½ ounces) water-packed chunk tuna,
     drained**
  2 hard-cooked eggs, cut into wedges
  1 tomato, cut into wedges

Prepare Vinaigrette Dressing; set aside. Boil potatoes until tender. Slice and gently toss with ¼ cup dressing; chill. Toss beans with 2 tablespoons dressing; chill. Tear lettuce into bite-size pieces. Toss with onions and place on large serving dish. Arrange tuna in center, surround with beans and potatoes. Garnish with egg and tomato wedges. Serve with remaining Vinaigrette Dressing.

Vinaigrette Dressing

Makes 1¼ cups

  ¾ cup oil
  ½ cup white wine vinegar
  1 tablespoon chopped parsley
  2 teaspoons chives
  1 teaspoon basil
  ½ teaspoon dry mustard
  ¼ teaspoon pepper
  ⅛ teaspoon garlic powder

Combine all ingredients; mix well.

Layered Vegetable Salad

Makes 10 servings

      6 cups chopped iceberg lettuce
      1 cup chopped red cabbage
      1 cup chopped red onion
      1 can (8 ounces) Chun King® Sliced Water Chest-
         nuts, drained
      1 can (17 ounces) Del Monte® Sweet Peas (No
         Salt Added), drained
      1 can (17 ounces) Del Monte® Whole Kernel Corn
         (No Salt Added), drained
      2 cups shredded carrots
      1 cup Mayonnaise (No Salt Added) (recipe
         follows)
      ½ cup sour cream
      2 tablespoons sugar (optional)

Place lettuce in 3-quart straight-sided dish or 13x9-inch serving dish. Top with layers of cabbage, onion, water chestnuts, peas, corn, and carrots. Combine mayonnaise with sour cream. Blend in sugar, if desired. Spread evenly over carrots. Cover tightly and refrigerate several hours for flavors to blend.

Mayonnaise (No Salt Added)

      2 egg yolks
      4 teaspoons fresh lemon juice
      ½ teaspoon dry mustard
      ¼ teaspoon onion powder
      ⅛ teaspoon garlic powder
      ¾ cup vegetable oil

Place egg yolks, lemon juice, mustard, onion, and garlic powder in blender or food processor container. Cover and process until well blended. Continue blending and gradually add oil in a thin stream to form emulsion.

Celery Rémoulade

Makes 4 servings

      2 bunches celery hearts
      2 tablespoons lemon juice
      2½ teaspoons salt, divided
      4 tablespoons Dijon-style prepared mustard
      ⅓ teaspoon white pepper
      3 tablespoons boiling water
      ⅓ cup olive oil
      2 to 3 tablespoons white wine vinegar
         Salad greens
      3 tablespoons minced parsley
      2 teaspoons minced chives

Wash and dry celery. Cut into small julienne strips. Place in a bowl; add lemon juice and 2 teaspoons salt. Mix well and let stand at room temperature 1 hour. To make dressing, warm the large bowl of Sunbeam Mixmaster Mixer by rinsing with hot water; dry. Place mustard and pepper in bowl. With mixer at medium low, add the boiling water, a few drops at a time. Continue to beat, adding the oil 1 or 2 drops at a time. Add 2 tablespoons vinegar and more seasoning, if necessary. Mix dressing gently with marinated celery. Cover; refrigerate overnight. When ready to serve, place salad greens on 4 salad plates, divide celery among the plates, and sprinkle with parsley and chives.

Cucumber Salad

Makes 3 to 4 servings

      2 cucumbers, thinly sliced
      ½ cup bottled Italian dressing
      1½ teaspoons Lea & Perrins Worcestershire Sauce

Combine all ingredients. Toss, cover, and chill.

Balkan Cucumbers

Makes 4 to 6 servings

      2 cups unflavored yogurt
      ½ clove garlic, mashed
      1 tablespoon white vinegar
      1½ teaspoons salt
      1 tablespoon olive oil
      1 tablespoon snipped chives
      1 teaspoon chopped mint leaves or ½ teaspoon
         dried mint
      1½ cups peeled, seeded, diced cucumber
      1 cup seedless green grape halves

Place yogurt in large Sunbeam Mixmaster Mixer bowl. Beat at medium until very smooth. Add garlic, vinegar, salt, olive oil, chives, and mint leaves; beat ½ minute. Fold in cucumber and grape halves. Refrigerate at least 1 hour before serving. Serve in salad bowls.

Layered Vegetable Salad. Del Monte Corporation

Simply Dilly Cucumbers

Makes about 24 cucumber spears
- ½ cup Wish-Bone® Italian Dressing
- ½ cup sour cream
- 2 tablespoons chopped fresh dill or 1 teaspoon dried dill weed
- 4 medium cucumbers, peeled and sliced in spears (about 1½ pounds)

In small bowl, blend Wish-Bone Italian Dressing, sour cream, and dill. Lay cucumber spears in large covered container, add dressing mixture, and toss; secure cover tightly and chill, tossing spears occasionally, 4 hours or overnight. Store in refrigerator for up to 1 week.

Wilted Cucumber Salad

Makes 4 to 6 servings
- 2 large cucumbers (about 1 pound each), pared
- 2 teaspoons salt
- 3 tablespoons sugar
- ½ cup Heinz Salad Vinegar
- ⅓ cup onion rings
  Pimiento strips

Score cucumbers with fork; thinly slice. Arrange cucumbers in layers in bowl, sprinkling each layer with salt. Weigh cucumbers down with smaller bowl; refrigerate several hours. Drain cucumbers well, squeezing out any excess liquid. Stir sugar into vinegar until dissolved; pour over cucumbers and onion rings. Cover; refrigerate at least 1 hour, turning occasionally. Serve as a salad or as a meat accompaniment. Garnish with pimiento strips.

When You're Dressing Up

It is the salad dressing that adds character to a salad. In choosing a dressing, remember that it should complement the ingredients and the flavor, not overpower them.

Try different types of dressings. Experiment with different oils and vinegars. Substitute lemon juice or lime juice for the vinegar, or mix them together. Change the herb from oregano to thyme or marjoram; switch from basil to tarragon, or add a touch of nutmeg or allspice.

Whatever ingredients you choose to combine in your dressing, keep in mind that the blender will make quick work of mixing them; it will also help to hold the flavors and the body together. Make enough to store in the refrigerator for later use.

Avoid the use of too much dressing—it will cause a salad to wilt. A general rule of thumb is to use ¼ cup of dressing to each 1½ quarts of greens.

Add dressing just before serving unless marinating.

French Quarter Lima Bean Salad

Makes 6 servings
- 1½ cups large lima beans, cooked or canned
- 1 hard-cooked egg
- ½ cup diced celery
- 3 tablespoons sliced dill pickle
- 1 cup mayonnaise
- 2 teaspoons lemon juice
- 2 teaspoons prepared mustard
  Dash hot pepper sauce
- 1 tablespoon chopped parsley
  Salt
  Lettuce cups

Drain limas, rinse, and chill. Dice egg and combine with limas, celery, and pickle. Mix together mayonnaise, lemon juice, mustard, pepper sauce, and parsley, and blend with bean mixture. Salt to taste. Arrange lettuce cups on individual salad plates and spoon in salad mixture. Serve ice cold.

Lima Salad Gazpacho

Makes 6 to 8 servings
- 4 to 5 cups large lima beans, cooked or canned, drained
- 1½ cups French or Italian dressing (bottled or homemade)
- 2 or 3 large tomatoes
- ½ cucumber
- ½ green pepper
- ½ cup sliced celery
- ½ cup sliced green onions
- ½ teaspoon crumbled oregano
- ⅛ teaspoon powdered cumin
- ½ teaspoon garlic salt
- ½ teaspoon basil
  Lettuce

To beans, add 1 cup of dressing. Cover and chill. An hour before serving, prepare gazpacho topping as follows: Dice tomatoes, cucumber, and green pepper coarsely. Add celery and onion. Mix seasonings with the remaining half cup of dressing and add to vegetables, mixing lightly. Chill. To serve the salad, drain off excess marinade from the limas, heap them on a bed of lettuce in a bowl or on one side of cold platter. Spoon the gazpacho mixture over the beans as a garnish.

Lentil Raisin Salad

Makes 4 to 6 servings
 1 cup dry lentils
 1 teaspoon tarragon
 1 teaspoon salt
 ¼ cup lemon juice or white wine vinegar
 2 tablespoons olive oil
 1 medium-size tomato, coarsely chopped
 ¾ cup thinly sliced scallions
 ½ cup Sun-Maid® Seedless Raisins
 ¼ teaspoon freshly ground pepper
   Lettuce leaves
   Onion rings

Rinse the lentils and place in a large pot with 2 cups water and the tarragon and salt; bring to a boil. Reduce heat, cover, and simmer for 25 to 30 minutes, or until the lentils are tender; drain well. Stir in the lemon juice, oil, tomato, scallions, raisins, and pepper. Mix gently and thoroughly. Cover and refrigerate for about 1 hour, or until the mixture is cool but not chilled. Spoon into a lettuce-lined plate and garnish with a few fresh onion rings.

Lettuce Wedges with Almond Honey-Mustard Mix

Makes 6 servings and 1½ cups dressing
 1 cup salad oil
 ¼ cup cider vinegar
 2 tablespoons Dijon-style mustard
 1 tablespoon Sue Bee Honey
 1 medium head iceberg lettuce
 ½ cup lightly toasted slivered almonds

Place all ingredients except lettuce and almonds in blender or food processor. Whirl for 1 minute in blender or until thoroughly mixed in food processor. To make salad, core lettuce, rinse and drain thoroughly. Cut into 6 wedges. Chill. Place on serving plates, spoon on dressing, and sprinkle with toasted almonds.

Wilted Lettuce

Makes 6 to 8 servings
 6 slices bacon
 ½ cup finely chopped onion
 ⅓ cup ReaLemon® Lemon Juice from Concentrate
 ⅓ cup water
 3 tablespoons sugar
 ½ head lettuce torn into bite-size pieces (about 6 cups)
   Salt and pepper

In a large skillet, fry bacon; remove and crumble, reserving drippings. Add onion; cook slightly. Stir in ReaLemon®, water, and sugar; heat thoroughly. Pour over lettuce; toss until wilted. Garnish with bacon; season to taste with salt and pepper.
Note: Gourmet cooks prefer lemon juice in salad dressing when they are serving wine; ReaLemon® won't compete with the wine or influence its bouquet.

Belgian Endive
Shaped like large, fat cigars, heads of Belgian endive (sometimes called witloof) are small and tightly closed, ivory at the root end shading to a delicate yellow-green at the tips of the blades.

With a somewhat bitter flavor that is likely to be an acquired taste, Belgian endive can add color and zest to mixed green salads (cut the heads across in thick slices, or separate into individual blades). Individual blades spread with a savory mixture, usually cheese-based, reassembled into the original head shape and chilled, then cut into thin slices, make a handsome and tasty garnish for meat, fish, or poultry salads.

Largely imported, Belgian endive is in the markets from October through May. It is sold by the pound, but you can determine the amount you need by the head—count on a head for 2 persons in a mixed salad.

Choose fresh, crisp-looking, tightly closed heads, without blemishes. Store in the refrigerator, in the vegetable crisper or a plastic bag, for no more than 5 days.

Low in calories, Belgian endive is a good source of vitamin A and a moderate source of iron.

Layered Onion-Pea Salad

Makes 6 servings
 1 large or 2 medium Idaho-Oregon Sweet Spanish Onions
 1 medium head lettuce, broken into chunks
 ¾ cup mayonnaise
 2 teaspoons sugar
 ½ teaspoon salt
 ⅛ teaspoon pepper
 1 package (10 ounces) frozen peas, cooked
 1 cup diced Swiss cheese
 3 slices bacon, cooked and crumbled
   Idaho-Oregon Sweet Spanish Onion rings

Remove skin from 1 large or 2 medium sweet Spanish onions. Slice thin and separate into rings to make about 3 cups. Place half of lettuce in salad bowl. Spoon half of mayonnaise over lettuce. Add a layer of onions and sprinkle with sugar, salt, and pepper. Top with half of peas and cheese. Repeat layers. Refrigerate 1 to 2 hours before serving. Garnish with crumbled bacon and onion rings.

Salad with Salsa Dressing

Makes 6 to 8 servings
    1 cup canned garbanzo beans
    1 cup cooked cut green beans
    1 cup cooked black beans
    1 cup cooked wax beans
    1 cup canned dark red kidney beans
    1 cup sliced carrots
    1 cup sliced celery
    1 small purple onion, sliced and separated into
        rings
    1 package (8 ounces) Pablos Mild Salsa
    ¼ cup oil
    2 tablespoons wine vinegar
    1 small clove garlic, minced
    ¼ teaspoon oregano, crushed
      Crisp salad greens

In bowl, combine first 8 ingredients. In measuring cup, combine salsa, oil, vinegar, garlic, and oregano. Blend well. Pour over vegetables. Toss to blend. Cover and refrigerate several hours or overnight. To serve, arrange on greens.

Picnic Special

Makes 6 servings
    6 all-beef frankfurters, cooked and sliced
    1 package (8 ounces) macaroni, cooked
    ½ cup diced green bell peppers
    ½ cup diced celery
    ½ cup mayonnaise
      Salt and pepper to taste
    2 tomatoes, cut in wedges
    3 hard-cooked eggs, cut in wedges

Combine cooked frankfurters with cooked macaroni. Add green peppers, celery, mayonnaise, salt, and pepper. Mix well and place in serving dish. Surround with tomato and egg wedges and chill thoroughly before serving.

Garbanzo Salad

Makes 4 cups
    1 can (15 ounces) garbanzo beans, drained
    2 cans (2¼ ounces each) sliced ripe olives,
        drained
    1 cup chopped green pepper
    ⅔ cup chopped Bermuda onion
    ¾ cup Tangy Tomato-Herb Dressing (recipe
        follows)

Toss all ingredients except dressing in a large bowl. Add dressing and toss until well mixed. Cover; refrigerate 2 to 3 hours before serving.

Garbanzo Salad. Photograph was provided by Hunt-Wesson Foods, Inc.; photography by Tom Kelley Studios

Tangy Tomato-Herb Dressing

Makes 2⅔ cups
    ¾ cup red wine vinegar
    ⅓ cup firmly packed brown sugar
    1 teaspoon onion powder
    ¾ teaspoon oregano
    ½ teaspoon *each* celery seed, dill weed, paprika,
        and salt
    ¼ teaspoon *each* garlic powder and basil
      Dash pepper
    1¼ cups pure vegetable oil
    1 can (6 ounces) Hunt's Tomato Paste

In a medium saucepan, bring vinegar, sugar, and spices to a boil. Cool 10 minutes. Add oil and Hunt's Tomato paste. Stir or beat until creamy. Refrigerate. Mix before using.

Salad with Salsa Dressing. Hernke Foods, Inc.

Gazpacho Relish Salad

Makes about 4 cups

   ⅓ **cup Wish-Bone® Italian Dressing**
   ¼ **cup tomato sauce**
      Hot pepper sauce
   4 **green onions, finely chopped**
   1 **medium green pepper, cut into thin strips**
   1 **medium cucumber, sliced**
   1 **medium tomato, cut into wedges**
   1 **cup bias-cut celery**

In small bowl, blend Wish-Bone Italian Dressing, tomato sauce, hot pepper sauce, and green onions. In 1-quart jar, layer green pepper, cucumber, tomato, and celery, adding ¼ dressing mixture between each layer; secure lid tightly and chill, inverting jar occasionally, 8 hours or overnight. Store in refrigerator for up to 1 week.

The Cook as Artist

Composed salads in the making are exceedingly satisfying to the artist that lurks in the soul of every cook; as ornaments for a party meal, particularly a buffet, they justify every moment (surprisingly, not as much time as they look to have taken) that is spent on them. And in the eating, they are gustatory delights.

What's a composed salad? A handsome, well-thought-out arrangement of any of dozens of ingredients, in good looks/taste combinations—a kind of edible free-style art form, one of the high points of the craft of making food beautiful. Generally, "the bigger the better" is a composed-salad guideline—one of the reasons they're so good for large-crowd buffets. Use your imagination in choosing the container. A big platter is fine. So is a tray of almost any shape. Offbeat containers work well, too—a giant-size plant saucer; a large shallow basket (line the bottom with plastic wrap); the bottom third sliced from a big pumpkin; a Mexican metate (the stone on which corn is ground to make the flour for tortillas); or almost anything else that comes to mind and to hand that is large, shallow, and offers a reasonably flat surface.

Here are some compositions to try—then let your imagination guide you. In all cases, be sure to provide serving utensils so guests can help themselves.

Tricolor Salad: Choose a long, rather narrow container; line it with leaves of Boston lettuce. Arrange thin slices of cooked beet, peeled orange, and Bermuda onion as your fancy dictates—in rows of alternating slices, in separate rows, however you choose. Provide a separate bowl of sour cream to use as dressing.

Garden Bounty: Plan to make this only when fresh basil and garden-fresh beefsteak tomatoes are in season. Line the container with watercress. Arrange tomato slices in an attractive pattern, overlapping them slightly. Combine 3 parts salt, 1 part coarsely ground black pepper, and 1 part sugar. Sprinkle the tomatoes with the mixture and let them stand at room temperature for 15 minutes. Sprinkle the tomatoes thickly with chopped fresh basil and drizzle olive or salad oil lightly over them. For many, the salad will require no further dressing; you might provide a cruet of red wine vinegar for those who want to add a touch of tartness.

Buona Festa Platter

Makes 8 to 10 servings
- 2 cups (16 ounces) Wish-Bone® Italian Dressing
- 1 can (16 ounces) whole green beans, drained
- 1 can (14 ounces) whole artichoke hearts, drained and halved (optional)
- 1 can (15 ounces) asparagus spears, drained
- 1 can (8¼ ounces) whole beets, drained
- 1 can (8 ounces) sliced carrots, drained
- 1 can (4 ounces) whole mushrooms, drained

Marinate each vegetable in a separate bowl as follows: Pour ½ cup Wish-Bone Italian Dressing over green beans and artichoke hearts; pour ¼ cup over asparagus, beets, carrots, and mushrooms. Cover and marinate in refrigerator, turning occasionally, 4 hours or overnight. To serve, arrange vegetables on platter.

Greek Salad with Cheese Rolls

Makes 6 servings
- 6 sheets phyllo dough
- 1 package (11 ounces) Montrachet or other goat cheese, cut into 6 equal pieces
- ⅓ cup melted butter or margarine
- 1 cup *each* cut-up zucchini, carrots, and radishes; bean sprouts; thinly sliced fennel; and slivered pea pods
- ¾ cup olive oil
- ¼ cup red wine vinegar
- 1 teaspoon salt
- ¼ teaspoon pepper
- ½ teaspoon oregano
- 1 tablespoon Dijon-style mustard
- 1 tablespoon sesame seed

Preheat oven to 400°F. Fold each sheet of phyllo dough in half lengthwise. Place cheese pieces at 1 short side. Turn in sides lengthwise. Brush dough with butter. Roll up jelly roll fashion, brushing with butter at every turn. Bake for 15 to 20 minutes, or until brown. Place cheese rolls on serving plates and surround with mounds of vegetables. In a mixing bowl, combine oil, vinegar, salt, pepper, oregano, and sesame seed and beat until thick. Spoon dressing over vegetables. Serve while cheese is warm.

Marinated Vegetable Salad

Makes 6 to 8 servings
- 1 cup bottled Italian salad dressing
- 3 tablespoons Lea & Perrins Worcestershire Sauce
- 1 package (10 ounces) frozen cauliflower, cooked and drained
- 1 package (9 ounces) frozen cut green beans, cooked and drained
- 2 cups sliced zucchini
- 1 green pepper, cut into strips
- 1 red pepper, cut into strips
- 1 can (3½ ounces) pitted ripe olives, drained

Combine salad dressing and Lea & Perrins; set aside. In a large bowl, combine cauliflower, green beans, zucchini, green pepper, red pepper, and olives. Pour salad dressing over vegetables. Toss well. Cover and refrigerate until chilled, about 1 hour, stirring occasionally.

Vegetable Salad Zip

Makes 1 quart

- 1 can (8 ounces) sliced carrots
- 1 can (16 ounces) whole green beans
- 1 can (8 ounces) whole-kernel corn
- 1 cup thinly sliced red onion
- ½ cup pitted ripe olives
- ¼ cup Sue Bee Honey
- ¼ cup salad oil
- ¼ cup wine vinegar
- ½ tablespoon salt (or to taste)
- ¼ teaspoon oregano
- ¼ teaspoon freshly ground pepper

Drain all vegetables. Combine all ingredients and chill, turning occasionally.

Citrus-Vegetable Medley

Makes about 3 cups

- ½ cup Wish-Bone® Italian Dressing
- ½ teaspoon marjoram
- 1 cup cooked cut green beans
- 1 cup cooked sliced carrots
- 1 cup cooked peas
- 1 small orange, thinly sliced
- ½ lemon, thinly sliced

In small bowl, combine Wish-Bone Italian Dressing and marjoram. In 1-quart jar, layer green beans, carrots, and peas with orange and lemon slices, adding ⅓ dressing mixture between each layer. Secure lid tightly and chill, inverting jar occasionally, 4 hours or overnight. Store in refrigerator for up to 1 week.

Carrot-Raisin Salad

Makes 4 servings

- 4 large carrots, pared and cut up
- ½ cup seedless raisins
- ½ teaspoon salt
  Dash pepper
- ½ to ¾ cup Sour Cream Dressing (see index)

Put carrots in blender container. Add cold water to cover. Cover; blend at medium speed just until carrots are chopped. Drain thoroughly in colander. Empty into bowl. Add raisins, salt, and pepper. Toss with Sour Cream Dressing.

Perky Patio Salad with Kikko Pecan Dressing

Makes 8 servings

- 3 medium tomatoes
- 1 large head lettuce, rinsed and drained
- 4 stalks celery, sliced
- 4 green onions and tops, cut diagonally into thin slices
- 1 small zucchini, cut into julienne strips
  Kikko Pecan Dressing (recipe follows)

Cut tomatoes into wedges; set aside. Tear lettuce into bite-size pieces; combine with tomatoes, celery, green onions, and zucchini in large salad bowl. Pour desired amount of Kikko Pecan Dressing over salad; toss to combine. Serve immediately.

Kikko Pecan Dressing

Makes about 2 cups

- 1 cup vegetable oil
- ¾ cup pecan halves or pieces
- ½ cup cider vinegar
- ¼ cup Kikkoman Soy Sauce
- 3 tablespoons minced fresh parsley
- 1 teaspoon sugar
- ½ teaspoon garlic powder

Place all ingredients in screw-top jar; cover and shake well to combine. Refrigerate 4 hours or overnight for flavors to blend. Shake thoroughly before serving.

Tossed Swiss and Mushroom Salad

Makes about 6 servings

- Dressing (recipe follows)
- 4 cups mixed salad greens, cut into bite-size pieces
- 1 cup sliced mushrooms
- 1 cup cubed Swiss cheese
- ½ cup walnut halves
- ⅓ cup Bac*Os imitation bacon

Prepare Dressing; toss with remaining ingredients.

Dressing

- ¼ cup plus 2 tablespoons vegetable oil
- 2 tablespoons white wine vinegar
- 1 teaspoon prepared mustard
- ⅛ teaspoon salt
- ⅛ teaspoon freshly ground pepper

Shake all ingredients in tightly covered container.

Potato Salad Guadalajara

Makes 4 servings

    1 package (5.5 ounces) Idaho® Dehydrated Au
        Gratin Potatoes with Sauce Mix
3⅔ cups water, divided
    3 tablespoons cider vinegar
    1 teaspoon chili powder
½ teaspoon ground cumin
    1 medium tomato, coarsely chopped
    1 avocado, seeded and coarsely chopped

In medium saucepan, combine potatoes and 3 cups water; heat to boiling. Reduce heat; cover; simmer 15 minutes until tender. Drain. Cool. Meanwhile, in small saucepan, combine sauce mix, remaining ⅔ cup water, vinegar, chili powder, and cumin. Cook, stirring constantly, until mixture boils and thickens. Cool to room temperature. In large bowl, combine potatoes, tomato, avocado, and sauce mixture; toss lightly. Cover. Chill.

Guido's Potato Salad

Makes 4 servings

    1 package (5.25 ounces) Idaho® Dehydrated
        Scalloped Potatoes with Sauce Mix
3¾ cups water, divided
    2 tablespoons vegetable oil
½ cup chopped onion
    1 clove garlic, minced
1½ teaspoons dried basil, crumbled
⅛ teaspoon pepper
    3 tablespoons wine vinegar
    1 medium-size red pepper, seeded and cut in
        julienne strips
½ cup sliced pitted black olives
    4 hard-cooked eggs, divided

In medium saucepan, combine potatoes and 3 cups water; heat to boiling. Reduce heat, cover, simmer until tender, about 15 minutes. Drain. Cool. Meanwhile, in small saucepan, heat oil; sauté onion and garlic until tender. Stir in sauce mix, basil, and pepper. Gradually add remaining ¾ cup water and vinegar. Cook, stirring constantly, until mixture boils and thickens. Cool to room temperature. In large bowl, combine sauce mixture, potatoes, red pepper, and olives. Coarsely chop 2 hard-cooked eggs; add to potatoes; toss gently. Cover. Chill. To serve, turn into serving dish; garnish with remaining 2 hard-cooked eggs, cut in wedges.

Potato Salad Guadalajara; Guido's Potato Salad; Red Sun Potato Salad.
Idaho Potato Commission

Red Sun Potato Salad

Makes 6 servings

½ cup vegetable oil, divided
    4 cups Idaho® Frozen Southern-Style Hash
        Brown Potatoes
    3 tablespoons soy sauce
    2 tablespoons cider vinegar
    1 tablespoon toasted sesame seed
¾ teaspoon ground ginger
¼ teaspoon pepper
    2 cups bean sprouts
1½ cups sliced mushrooms
½ cup finely sliced scallions

In large skillet, heat ¼ cup oil; carefully add potatoes to form a single layer. Cover. Cook 8 to 10 minutes, stirring occasionally, until potatoes are done. Cool. In small bowl, combine remaining ¼ cup oil, soy sauce, vinegar, sesame seed, ginger, and pepper; mix well. In large bowl, combine potatoes, bean sprouts, mushrooms, scallions, and soy sauce mixture; toss lightly. Cover. Chill.

Old-Fashioned Potato Salad

Makes about 4 cups

½ cup Hellmann's or Best Foods Real Mayonnaise
½ cup minced onion
    1 tablespoon white vinegar
    1 teaspoon salt
⅛ teaspoon pepper
    1 hard-cooked egg, chopped
1½ pounds potatoes (about 3 cups), cooked, peeled,
        and cubed
    1 cup sliced celery
        Paprika

In medium bowl, stir together first 6 ingredients. Add potatoes and celery; toss to coat well. Cover; chill at least 4 hours. Sprinkle with paprika.

Q. *Are snow peas and Chinese pea pods the same thing? How should they be cooked—both the fresh and the frozen kinds?*
A. They are the same thing, and you can find them frozen (alone or with water chestnuts) all year around, and fresh in produce markets and Chinese specialty food shops during the summer. However you cook them, fresh or frozen, make it brief. Place in a skillet with ¼ inch boiling water and a little butter, return to boil and simmer no more than 2 minutes. Serve hot with butter or hollandaise sauce, or chill and add to salads. Or add, uncooked, to stir-fry dishes 2 or 3 minutes before the dish is finished.

Cucumber Potato Salad

Makes 4 to 6 servings
    1 package (5.5 ounces) Idaho® Au Gratin Potatoes
3½ cups water, divided
    2 tablespoons lemon juice
    ¼ teaspoon salt
    ¼ teaspoon dried tarragon
    1 tablespoon chopped fresh dill or 1 teaspoon
        dried dill weed
    ½ cup sour cream
    ¼ cup milk
    ¼ cup chopped onion
    1 cucumber, pared, seeded, and chopped

Remove sauce packet from potatoes. Heat 3 cups water to boiling in medium saucepan. Add potatoes, cover, and simmer 12 minutes, just until potatoes are tender. Drain and rinse with cold water; drain well. In large skillet, blend remaining ½ cup water, lemon juice, and seasoning packet. Add salt, tarragon, and dill; stir over medium heat until mixture thickens and comes to a boil. Stir in sour cream and milk. In large bowl, combine potatoes, onion, cucumber, and dressing; mix well. Cover and refrigerate until chilled.

Jiffy Potato and Egg Salad

Makes 4 to 6 servings
    1 package (5.5 ounces) Idaho® Hash Brown
        Potatoes
1¾ cups boiling water
    ½ cup chopped celery
    ¼ cup chopped scallions
    3 hard-cooked eggs, peeled and chopped
    1 tablespoon chopped parsley
    ½ cup mayonnaise
    ¼ cup milk
    1 tablespoon prepared mustard
    1 teaspoon salt
    ¼ teaspoon pepper
        Dash cayenne

Place hash brown potatoes in mixing bowl; pour boiling water over potatoes and let stand until water is absorbed, about 10 minutes. Add remaining ingredients and mix well. Cover and refrigerate until serving time.

Sweet Potato Salad

Makes 6 to 8 servings
3½ pounds orange sweet potatoes
        Salted water
    1 medium onion, cut into thin rings
    1 green pepper, cut into thin strips
        Honey Vinaigrette Dressing (recipe follows)

Wash sweet potatoes. Heat enough salted water to boiling to cover sweet potatoes. Add sweet potatoes in jackets; bring back to boil, cover, and cook 20 to 30 minutes, or until just fork-tender. Do not overcook. When cool enough to handle, halve lengthwise; then cut into ¼-inch slices. Combine sweet potato slices, onion rings, and green pepper strips in large bowl. Pour Honey Vinaigrette Dressing over salad mixture. Toss lightly to coat vegetables. Cover and refrigerate 3 to 6 hours or overnight. Serve chilled or at room temperature.

Honey Vinaigrette Dressing

    1 cup tarragon vinegar
    ½ cup vegetable oil
    1 tablespoon honey
    2 cloves garlic, minced or pressed
    2 bay leaves, crumbled
    ½ teaspoon salt
    ¼ teaspoon pepper
    ¼ teaspoon *each* oregano and thyme, crumbled

Combine all ingredients in jar with tight-fitting lid. Shake vigorously until well mixed.

Speedy Potato Salad

Makes about 10 servings
    3 cans (16 ounces each) sliced potatoes, drained
        and rinsed
    1 cup sliced celery
    2 tablespoons chopped onion
    ½ cup sour cream
    ¼ cup Wish-Bone® Italian Dressing

In bowl, combine potatoes, celery, and onion; toss with sour cream blended with Wish-Bone Italian Dressing and chill.

Sweet Potatoes for Salads

Wash and peel sweet potato. Grate or use a potato peeler for taking off thin strips or curls for decorating or mixing into fresh salad. To ensure crispness, keep strips or curls in ice water (with or without salt) until ready to use.

Savory Potato Salad

Makes 6 servings

  6 medium-size potatoes, cooked and peeled
  ½ teaspoon savory
  ¼ teaspoon marjoram
  2 teaspoons salt
  ¼ teaspoon pepper
  1 tablespoon caraway seed
  ¼ cup salad oil
  ¼ cup cider vinegar
  1 medium-size onion, minced
  ½ cup mayonnaise
  2 teaspoons Grey Poupon Mustard
  3 hard-cooked eggs, shelled
    Lettuce leaves
    Tomato quarters

Slice or dice potatoes into a large bowl. Put seasonings into a jar with the oil and vinegar; shake to blend well. Pour mixture over the potatoes and let stand about 1 hour. Add onion, mayonnaise, and mustard. Dice 2 of the hard-cooked eggs and add to the potato mixture. Toss gently to combine all ingredients thoroughly. Serve on lettuce leaves and garnish with tomato quarters and remaining egg, sliced.

Hot Potato Salad

Makes 8 servings

  8 medium potatoes (about 3 pounds)
  1 packet Herb-Ox Onion Flavored Instant Broth
    and Seasoning
  3 slices bacon
1½ tablespoons all-purpose flour
  1 teaspoon dry mustard
  ⅓ cup vinegar
    Salt and pepper
  2 scallions, minced

Cover peeled potatoes with boiling water; add instant broth; cook until tender. Drain and slice potatoes. Reserve ⅔ cup cooking liquid. Fry bacon until crisp, drain on paper towels, crumble. Remove pan from heat, add flour and dry mustard to bacon fat. Add vinegar and potato liquid; cook over low heat, stirring, until smooth and thickened. Adjust seasoning with salt and pepper. Sprinkle potatoes with scallions and dressing, toss gently to mix. Serve hot.

Vinegar Varieties

The three principal types of vinegar available to us in our markets are cider, distilled, and wine. A fourth, malt vinegar, is not as widely used, but seems to be gaining in popularity—perhaps with the increasing popularity of fish and chips, which are properly eaten sprinkled with malt vinegar. Flavored vinegars can be made by adding various taste-enhancing elements to any of these vinegars.

Cider vinegar: This type is the most commonly used. It is made by fermenting apple cider, and has an acetic acid content of from 5 to 6 percent. A pale gold-brown in color, it has a flavor that speaks of the apples used in its making.

Distilled vinegar: This is the one we refer to—and recipes call for—as white vinegar. It contains 5 to 12 percent acetic acid, is made by fermenting a dilute solution of alcohol distilled from grain mash. Colorless, it has no flavor of the grain from which it was made, which is eliminated in the distillation.

Wine vinegar: This can be made from any of the 3 broad classifications of wine—red, white, or rosé. Like cider vinegar, its acetic acid content is 5 to 6 percent. The color and flavor reflect the type of wine used.

Malt vinegar: This is made from barley malt and, like good wines, is aged before it is put on the market. Russet-brown in color, it is definitely aromatic and has a distinctive flavor that some enjoy, others feel is too assertive.

Flavored vinegars: The most common additives used to flavor vinegar—most often wine vinegar—are tarragon, basil, and garlic. Such flavored vinegars can be made at home. Crush the garlic clove or bruise the herbs and add to a bottle of red or white wine vinegar. Let stand for 3 days, then strain the vinegar and return it to its bottle.

A wide variety of salad dressings and sauces depend on vinegar for their delightful flavor. We use it in smaller amounts to perk up the flavors of many foods, as well as a preservative in relishes and all sorts of pickled foods.

Cabbage Slaw

Makes 6 servings

1 medium head green cabbage, cored and
    coarsely cut up
1 cup Sour Cream Dressing (see index)

Put cabbage into blender container to 5-cup mark; add water just to cover. Cover; blend at medium speed just until chopped. Drain thoroughly in colander; empty into large bowl. Repeat process with remaining cabbage. Toss with Sour Cream Dressing.

Red Cabbage Slaw

Substitute 1 medium head red cabbage for green cabbage, or use half red cabbage and half green cabbage. Proceed as for Cabbage Slaw.

Calico Slaw

Substitute ½ red cabbage and ½ green cabbage for medium head green cabbage. Add 2 carrots, cut up, and ½ small onion, cut up. Proceed as for Cabbage Slaw.

Blend 'n' Gel Coleslaw

Makes 8 servings

2 envelopes Knox® Unflavored Gelatine
½ cup cold water
1 cup boiling water
1 teaspoon salt
2 tablespoons lemon juice
1 cup mayonnaise
1 medium onion, quartered
2 cups cabbage pieces
1 cup celery pieces
1 cup peeled cucumber pieces

In a 5-cup blender container, sprinkle Knox Unflavored Gelatine over cold water. Let stand 3 to 4 minutes. Add boiling water; cover and process at low speed 2 minutes. Add salt, lemon juice, and mayonnaise; process until well blended. Stop blender and add onion; process at high speed until finely chopped. Stop blender and add cabbage, celery, and cucumber pieces; cover and process at high speed only until coarsely chopped. Turn into a 6-cup bowl and chill until firm, 2 to 3 hours.

Calico Slaw. Hamilton Beach Scovill Inc.

Q. *Recipes often say to peel and seed cucumbers, which is a big nuisance. Now I've come across a recipe that tells me to peel and seed tomatoes. How?*

A. First the cucumber. Cut off both ends, then take off the thinnest possible layer of skin with a swivel-blade vegetable peeler. Cut in half lengthwise. Now your tool is a teaspoon. Slip the tip under the seed mass at one end and push, zipping the seeds out all at once in no time.

Spear a tomato with a long-handled fork at the stem end. Hold over the lighted burner of a gas stove until the skin sputters and cracks, at which point you can easily peel it off in big pieces. Or drop into boiling water for one minute, then peel the same way—and as easily. With a sharp knife, cut out the stem and core in a cone-shaped piece. With your hands, squeeze out seeds and the juice that surrounds them.

Hot Honey Coleslaw

Makes 6 servings

1 small head cabbage, shredded
3 tablespoons butter or margarine
¼ teaspoon salt
    Freshly ground pepper to taste
¼ cup wine vinegar
1 teaspoon caraway seed
2 tablespoons Sue Bee Honey

Put shredded cabbage in saucepan with just enough water to cover bottom of pan. Cover and cook 6 to 7 minutes, or until crisp-tender. Drain thoroughly. Add butter and toss to melt and coat cabbage. Season with salt, pepper, vinegar, caraway seed, and Sue Bee Honey. Toss gently and continue cooking over very low heat until well blended. Taste and adjust seasoning.

Hawaiian Slaw

Makes about 8 servings

⅔ cup Wish-Bone® Russian Dressing
1 small head cabbage, shredded
1 can (8¼ ounces) pineapple chunks, drained
1 orange, diced
¼ cup chopped green pepper

In large bowl, combine all ingredients; chill.

San Joaquin Glamour Fig Slaw

Makes 5 or 6 servings

- 1 medium-size solid head cabbage
- 12 California dried figs, stewed and drained
- 2 fresh carrots
- 2 tablespoons onion, grated
- 2 sprigs parsley
- 1 teaspoon celery seed
- 1 can (10½ ounces) crushed pineapple, including syrup
- 3 tablespoons mayonnaise
- 2 tablespoons sugar
- 1 teaspoon salt
- 1 teaspoon freshly ground pepper
- ½ teaspoon dry mustard
- 3 tablespoons vinegar
- ½ cup heavy cream
  Additional stewed figs
  Lettuce leaves

Wash the cabbage, remove blemished leaves. Cut stem at bottom to make even base. Cut out center of cabbage. Scoop out all possible cabbage, but retain a good shell that will not leak. Remove stems from figs. Then put scooped-out cabbage, figs, carrots, onion, and parsley through food grinder, using the coarse blade. Add all the remaining ingredients except the cream. Stir together lightly. Whip the cream and fold into the salad. Spoon into cabbage shell, heaping high. Garnish with more stewed figs and small lettuce leaves. Adjust seasoning to your own taste, if desired.

Carrot-Currant Slaw

Makes 4 servings

- 1 can (8 ounces) crushed pineapple
- 1 tablespoon cornstarch
- ¼ teaspoon dry mustard
- ¼ teaspoon salt
- 2 tablespoons cider vinegar
- 2 tablespoons mayonnaise
- 2 cups shredded peeled carrots
- ½ cup Sun-Maid® Zante Currants
- 4 lettuce cups

In medium-size saucepan, combine the pineapple, cornstarch, mustard, and salt. Cook over medium heat, stirring constantly, until the mixture boils and thickens. Remove from heat. Stir in the vinegar and refrigerate until well chilled. Gently stir in the mayonnaise. Mix the carrots and currants in a bowl. Spoon into lettuce cups and serve on individual salad plates.

Waldorf Slaw

Makes abut 14 servings

- 5 cups shredded cabbage
- 2 cups diced apple
- ⅓ cup raisins
- ½ cup mayonnaise
- ¼ cup Wish-Bone® Sweet 'n Spicy French Dressing

In large bowl, combine cabbage, apple, and raisins; toss with mayonnaise and Wish-Bone Sweet 'n Spicy French Dressing.

Islander Coleslaw

Makes about 8 servings

- 3 cups shredded cabbage
- 1 cup shredded carrots
- ½ cup chopped green pepper
- ⅓ cup Wish-Bone® Thousand Island Dressing
- 1 tablespoon lemon juice
- 1 tablespoon Worcestershire sauce (optional)

In medium bowl, combine all ingredients; chill.

Crunchy Baby Lima and Cheddar Slaw

Makes 4 to 6 servings

- 3 cups shredded cabbage
- 1 tablespoon minced green onion
- ⅛ teaspoon garlic salt
  Creamy Dressing (recipe follows)
- 1 red apple, unpeeled, cored, and diced
- 1 tablespoon lemon juice
- 1⅔ cups drained, cooked, or canned white baby lima beans
- 4 ounces cheddar cheese, cubed
  Romaine lettuce leaves

Combine cabbage, onion, and garlic salt; add ¼ cup Creamy Dressing and toss lightly. Sprinkle apple with lemon juice. Combine cabbage mixture, beans, apple, and cheese in a salad bowl and mix well with a little more dressing, if needed to coat all ingredients. Edge the bowl with romaine leaves spears and offer to guests for self service.

Creamy Dressing

- 1 cup sour cream
- ¼ cup mayonnaise
- 2 tablespoons vinegar
- 1 teaspoon sugar
- ¼ teaspoon Worcestershire sauce
- ¼ teaspoon celery seed (optional)

Combine all ingredients and mix well.

Perfection Salad

Makes 4 to 6 servings
 1 package (4-serving size) lemon-flavored gelatin
 1 cup boiling water
 ¾ cup pineapple juice
 1 medium carrot, pared and cut up
 1 cup coarsely cut cabbage
 1 tablespoon lemon juice
 ½ teaspoon salt
   Salad greens

Put gelatin and boiling water into blender container. Cover; blend at low speed until gelatin is dissolved. Add remaining ingredients except salad greens to blender container in order listed. Cover; blend at medium speed just until vegetables are chopped. Chill until slightly thickened. Stir gently to disperse vegetables. Pour into 3-cup mold or into individual molds. Chill until firm. Unmold onto salad greens.

Carrot-Raisin Slaw

Makes 4 servings
 4 large carrots, pared and cut up
 ½ cup seedless raisins
 ½ teaspoon salt
   Dash pepper
 ½ to ¾ cup Sour Cream Dressing (recipe follows)

Put carrots into blender container. Add cold water to cover. Cover; blend at medium speed just until carrots are chopped. Drain thoroughly in colander. Empty into bowl. Add raisins, salt, and pepper. Toss with Sour Cream Dressing.

Sour Cream Dressing

Makes 2½ cups
 1¼ cups mayonnaise
 1 cup sour cream
 2 tablespoons lemon juice
   Dash hot pepper sauce

Put all ingredients into blender container in order listed. Cover; blend at high speed until smooth.

Dill Sour Cream Dressing
Add ⅛ teaspoon dry mustard and 4 sprigs fresh dill or ½ teaspoon dried dill weed. Proceed as for Sour Cream Dressing.

Slaw with Green Onions

Makes 6 servings
 3 cups shredded green cabbage
 ½ cup chopped parsley
 ¼ cup chopped green onions, including tops
 ¼ cup Sue Bee Honey
 1 teaspoon vegetable salt
 ¼ cup cider vinegar
 2 teaspoons safflower or sesame oil
   Sliced radishes or black olives

Combine cabbage, parsley, and green onions and refrigerate until cold. Combine Sue Bee Honey, salt, vinegar, and oil. Blend well and chill. Pour dressing over vegetables and toss lightly. Garnish with radishes or black olives.

Strassburg Slaw

Makes 6 servings
 ½ cup nuts
 3 cups cabbage, cut into pieces
 1 cup crushed pineapple, drained
 2 bananas, sliced
 ¼ cup mayonnaise
 ½ cup heavy cream

Place nuts in blender. Cover and process at Chop; empty into large bowl. Chop cabbage in same manner; add to nuts. Add pineapple and bananas to cabbage. Put mayonnaise and cream into blender; cover and process at Whip until thick. Fold into cabbage mixture. Chill before serving.

Crunchy Salad Additions

We know, of course, that we make slaw from cabbage. But thin-shredded cabbage, red or green—Chinese cabbage, too—makes an attractive and crunchy addition to a mixed green salad. So do these other vegetables, for variety's sake:
   hearts of palm (canned)
   white, kidney, or ceci beans (canned)
   artichoke hearts (cooked)
   sliced cucumber
   sliced water chestnuts or bamboo shoots
   thin-sliced raw turnip
   thin onion rings
   chopped celery stalks and leaves
   raw carrot (shredded or thin-sliced)
   bean or alfalfa sprouts
   sliced radishes

Fresh-as-Spring Asparagus Salad

Makes about 6 servings

1¼ pounds (about ½ bunch) fresh asparagus spears,
      cooked
   6 cherry tomatoes, halved
   6 tablespoons Wish-Bone® Italian Dressing
   2 envelopes Knox® Unflavored Gelatine
   2 tablespoons sugar
1½ cups boiling water
   1 cup mayonnaise
   3 tablespoons lemon juice
   1 cup chopped cherry tomatoes
1½ tablespoons finely chopped onion

Cut 6 asparagus spears into 4-inch lengths and marinate with cherry tomato halves in 2 tablespoons Wish-Bone Italian Dressing; marinate in refrigerator. Cut remaining asparagus into ½-inch pieces; reserve. In medium bowl, mix Knox Unflavored Gelatine and sugar; add boiling water and stir until gelatine is completely dissolved. With wire whisk or rotary beater, blend in mayonnaise, remaining Wish-Bone Italian Dressing, and lemon juice. Chill, stirring occasionally, until mixture is consistency of unbeaten egg whites. Fold in reserved asparagus pieces, chopped tomatoes, and onion; turn into 9-inch round baking pan and chill until firm, about 4 hours. Unmold and garnish, in spokelike pattern, with marinated asparagus spears and cherry tomato halves.

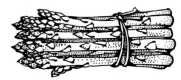

Crab Mousse in Tomato Cups (page 121); Potato Salad Crécy Mold (page 89); Sangría Fruit Salad (page 60). United Fresh Fruit & Vegetable Assn.

Fresh Mushroom-Cucumber Mold

Makes 8 servings

   2 envelopes Knox® Unflavored Gelatine
   ½ cup cold water
   2 cups boiling water
   1 bottle (8 ounces) Wish-Bone® Russian Dressing
      (regular or lite)
   1 cup sliced fresh mushrooms
   1 cup diced cucumber
   ½ cup sliced celery
   2 tablespoons thinly sliced green onions

In a medium bowl, mix Knox Unflavored Gelatine with cold water. Add boiling water and stir until gelatine is completely dissolved. Add Wish-Bone Russian Dressing; chill, stirring occasionally, until mixture is the consistency of unbeaten egg whites. Fold in remaining ingredients. Turn into a 5-cup mold; chill until firm. Unmold to serve.

Fresh-as-Spring Asparagus Salad. Photo courtesy of Thomas J. Lipton, Inc.

Garden Salad Mold

Makes 8 servings

   2 envelopes Knox® Unflavored Gelatine
   ½ cup cold water
2¼ cups boiling water
   ½ cup sugar or equivalent artificial sweetener
   ½ teaspoon salt
   ½ cup lemon juice
   ½ cup sliced radishes
   ½ cup grated carrot
   2 cups finely shredded cabbage
   ½ cup diced green pepper

In a medium bowl, mix Knox Unflavored Gelatine with cold water. Add boiling water and stir until gelatine is completely dissolved. Add sugar and salt; stir until dissolved. Stir in lemon juice. Chill, stirring occasionally, until mixture is the consistency of unbeaten egg whites. Fold in remaining ingredients. Turn into 8 individual molds; chill until firm. Unmold to serve.

Beet and Cucumber Relish Mold

Makes 4 to 6 servings
   1 package (4-serving size) lime- or lemon-
      flavored gelatin
 ¾ teaspoon salt
   1 can (16 ounces) sliced or diced beets
   1 thin slice onion
   1 tablespoon vinegar
   1 teaspoon prepared horseradish
 ⅔ cup cracked or crushed ice
 ½ medium cucumber, pared and cut up
      Salad greens

Put gelatin and salt into blender container. Drain liquid from beets; measure ¾ cup liquid; heat to boiling. Pour into blender container. Cover; blend at low speed until gelatin is dissolved. Add onion, vinegar, horseradish, and ice. Cover; blend at medium speed until ice is melted. Add cucumber and drained beets. Cover; blend at medium speed just until vegetables are coarsely chopped. Pour into 1-quart ring mold or individual molds. Chill until slightly thickened. Stir gently to disperse vegetables. Chill until firm. Unmold on salad greens.

Molded Cucumber Salad

Makes 6 to 8 servings
   1 small onion, halved
   1 stalk celery, cut in 4-inch lengths boiling water
   2 cups cottage cheese
   1 large cucumber, peeled and sliced
 ½ cup sour cream
   1 package (3 ounces) cream cheese, softened and
      cubed
   2 slices (½-inch thick each) onion
 ½ cup chopped celery
 ½ cup chopped walnuts
      Lettuce

Place gelatin and boiling water in blender container; cover. Grind 40 seconds. Add cottage cheese, cucumber, sour cream, cream cheese, and onion. Grind 30 seconds longer, stopping motor to push ingredients to blades. Stir in celery and nuts by hand. Pour into 6-cup mold. Chill until firm. To serve, unmold onto chilled lettuce-lined plate.

Vegetable Salad Italiano

Makes 8 servings
   1 small cucumber, diced
 12 cherry tomatoes, halved
   1 cup diced green pepper
   1 cup small cauliflowerets
 ½ cup Wish-Bone® Italian Dressing (regular or
      lite)
   2 envelopes Knox® Unflavored Gelatine
 ½ cup cold water
 1½ cups boiling water

In a large bowl, toss vegetables with Wish-Bone Italian Dressing; marinate in refrigerator overnight. In a medium bowl, mix Knox Unflavored Gelatine with cold water. Add boiling water and stir until gelatine is completely dissolved. Stir gelatine into vegetable mixture. Turn into a 6-cup mold; chill until firm. Unmold to serve.

Salad Greens Know-how

When you go to buy salad makings, be on the lookout for young and tender greens, free of dirt. (But dirt is by nature a part of some—often there's a muddy clump at the very heart of a head of Boston lettuce, for example.) Yellow, dry, or wilted leaves or those with brown edges proclaim that the green has outlived its usefulness. Store in separate plastic bags in the refrigerator's crisper.

Wash and store greens properly—as soon as they are brought home, wash, dry, and refrigerate them according to the following procedures:

• Remove and discard any outer leaves of a head of lettuce that are bruised. Cut out the core with a sharp knife or rap it sharply with the heel of your hand and pull it out; hold the head under cold running water so that it fills the cavity that once held the core. With greens such as escarole, chicory, and romaine, leave the root ends but wash the leaves thoroughly under cold running water.

• Shake excess water off greens and blot each leaf.

Store washed green leaves in a crisper in the refrigerator. If you plan to keep them for any length of time, place them in transparent plastic wrap, plastic bags, or a special airtight plastic container. Store watercress and parsley in tightly covered jars or sealed plastic bags after washing and drying them.

• If you're making green salad for a large group, wash and dry the greens a couple of hours before the party and add whatever else (except dressing) is going into the salad. Lay out a very large plastic bag and place a spread-out towel inside. Pile the salad on the towel, close the bag with a twister tie or pipe cleaner, and carefully, gently put the whole thing into the refrigerator, towel side down, until you're ready to dress the salad.

Potato Salad Crécy Mold

Makes 8 to 12 servings

  2 envelopes unflavored gelatin
  2 cups milk, divided
1¾ teaspoons salt
  ¾ teaspoon dry mustard
  ¼ teaspoon Tabasco pepper sauce
  1 tablespoon fresh lemon juice
  1 cup sour cream
  2 cups diced cooked potatoes
  1 cup grated carrot
  ½ cup chopped green pepper
  ½ cup chopped celery
  ¼ cup sliced scallions
  ¼ cup thinly sliced radishes
  2 tablespoons chopped parsley
  1 tablespoon snipped fresh dill weed
  ½ cup heavy cream, whipped
     Salad greens
     Carrot curls

Sprinkle gelatin over 1 cup milk in medium saucepan; let stand until gelatin is moistened. Place over low heat and stir constantly until gelatin dissolves, 4 or 5 minutes. Remove from heat. Stir in remaining 1 cup milk, salt, dry mustard, Tabasco sauce, and lemon juice. Add sour cream and beat until smooth. Chill, stirring occasionally, until mixture mounds slightly when dropped from a spoon. Fold in vegetables, parsley, and dill. Fold in whipped cream. Turn into a 6-cup mold and chill until firm, several hours or overnight. Unmold and garnish with salad greens and carrot curls.

Apple-Vegetable Salad Ring

Makes 8 servings

  2 envelopes unflavored gelatin
  ½ cup cold water
  2 cans (12 ounces each) ginger ale
  2 teaspoons Lea & Perrins Worcestershire Sauce
  ½ teaspoon salt
  1 cup diced celery
  1 cup diced apple
  1 cup shredded carrots

In a small saucepan, sprinkle gelatin over water; let stand 5 minutes to soften. Heat over low heat to dissolve; cool slightly. In a mixing bowl, combine gelatin with ginger ale, Lea & Perrins, and salt; chill until as thick as unbeaten egg whites. Stir in celery, apple, and carrots. Turn into a 6-cup ring mold. Chill until firm and ready to serve. Unmold onto a serving platter.

New-Day Gazpacho Salad

Makes 4 servings

  1 envelope Knox® Unflavored Gelatine
  ½ cup cold water
  1 envelope instant beef-flavor broth
  ¾ cup boiling water
  ¼ cup vinegar
  ½ teaspoon salt
  1 teaspoon paprika
  ½ teaspoon dried basil
  ⅛ teaspoon hot pepper sauce
  2 tablespoons chopped onion
  ¼ cup finely chopped celery
  ½ cup finely chopped green pepper
1½ cups chopped fresh tomatoes
     Lettuce leaves (optional)

In a medium bowl, mix Knox Unflavored Gelatine with cold water. Let stand 1 minute. Sprinkle broth powder over gelatine mixture. Add boiling water and stir until gelatine and broth are completely dissolved. Stir in vinegar, salt, paprika, basil, and hot pepper sauce. Chill, stirring occasionally, until mixture is the consistency of unbeaten egg whites. Fold in remaining ingredients. Turn into individual cups or molds. Chill until firm. Unmold onto lettuce leaves, if desired.

Cucumber Mousse

Makes 8 servings

  1 large or 2 small cucumbers
  1 envelope unflavored gelatin
  ¼ cup cold water
  2 tablespoons boiling water
  6 tablespoons mayonnaise
  1 teaspoon Worcestershire sauce
  1 teaspoon salt
     Dash white pepper
  1 cup creamed cottage cheese
     Green food coloring (optional)

Peel cucumber and cut into 1-inch pieces. Put into blender; cover and process at Purée until smooth. Reserve 1½ cups processed cucumber. Soften gelatin in cold water in blender; add boiling water. Cover and process at Stir until dissolved. Add 1½ cups cucumber and remaining ingredients. Process at Mix until smooth. If desired, tint the mixture a pale green with a few drops of food coloring. Pour into a 1-quart mold or into 8 individual molds. Cover and freeze. Defrost before serving.

Green Goddess Cucumber Cooler. Photo courtesy of
Thomas J. Lipton, Inc.

Good-Health Vegetable Salads 91

Green Goddess Cucumber Cooler

Makes 8 servings
    2 envelopes Knox® Unflavored Gelatine
    1 cup cold water
 1½ cups Wish-Bone® Green Goddess Dressing
    1 teaspoon instant minced onion
    ½ teaspoon salt
    1 teaspoon dried dill weed
    3 cups finely chopped cucumber
    ½ cup chopped celery
      Salad greens (optional)
      Cherry tomatoes (optional)

In a medium saucepan, mix Knox Unflavored Gelatine with cold water. Let stand 1 minute. Stir over
medium heat until gelatine is completely dissolved,
about 1 minute. Remove from heat; stir in Wish-Bone
Green Goddess Dressing, onion, salt, and dill weed.
Chill, stirring occasionally, until mixture is the consistency of unbeaten egg whites. Fold in cucumber and
celery. Turn into a 5-cup mold that has been lightly
brushed with additional dressing. Chill until firm. Unmold to serve. Garnish with salad greens and cherry
tomatoes, if desired.

New-Way Three-Bean Salad. Photo courtesy of Thomas J. Lipton,
Inc.

New-Way Three-Bean Salad

Makes 12 servings
    1 package (10 ounces) frozen lima beans, cooked and
      drained
    1 can (15 or 16 ounces) red kidney beans, drained
    1 can (16 to 20 ounces) garbanzo beans, drained
    ¼ cup chopped parsley
    ¼ teaspoon white pepper
    4 tablespoons cider vinegar, divided
 2½ teaspoons salt, divided
    3 envelopes Knox® Unflavored Gelatine
    2 teaspoons sugar
    ½ cup cold water
    4 cups boiling water
      Salad greens (optional)

In a large bowl, combine lima beans, kidney beans,
and garbanzos. Add parsley, pepper, 3 tablespoons vinegar, and 1½ teaspoons salt. Cover and refrigerate about
2 hours, tossing occasionally.

In a medium bowl, mix Knox Unflavored Gelatine
with sugar and ½ cup cold water. Add 4 cups boiling
water and stir until gelatine is completely dissolved. Stir
in remaining 1 tablespoon vinegar and 1 teaspoon salt.
Chill, stirring occasionally, until mixture is the consistency of unbeaten egg whites. Fold gelatine mixture into
bean mixture. Turn into individual molds or cups; chill
until firm. Unmold onto salad greens, if desired.

Red Russian Ring

Makes 6 to 8 servings
    2 envelopes Knox® Unflavored Gelatine
    3 cups tomato juice, divided
    ½ cup Wish-Bone® Russian Dressing
    1 cup finely chopped green pepper
    ½ cup finely chopped celery

In a large bowl, mix Knox Unflavored Gelatine with
½ cup cold tomato juice. Heat remaining 2½ cups
juice to boiling; add to gelatine mixture and stir until
gelatine is completely dissolved. Add Wish-Bone Russian Dressing. Chill, stirring occasionally, until mixture is the consistency of unbeaten egg whites. Fold in
green pepper and celery. Turn into a 5-cup ring mold
or bowl; chill until firm. Unmold to serve.
Idea: To turn this side-dish salad into a main-dish
delight, fill the center of the ring with an oniony egg-
salad mixture, or dress it up with cooked whole
shrimp, and send extra Wish-Bone Russian Dressing to
the table.

Sweet Potato Salad Mold

Makes 4 to 6 servings

    1 package (4-serving size) orange-flavored gelatin
 1½ cups boiling water
    1 small can crushed pineapple (reserve juice)
   ¼ cup fresh orange juice
    1 tablespoon grated orange peel
    1 tablespoon lemon juice
    1 teaspoon grated lemon peel
    1 cup mashed sweet potatoes
   ⅛ teaspoon ground cinnamon
      Topping (recipe follows)

Dissolve gelatin with boiling water and juice from pineapple. When cool, add other ingredients. Mix well. Pour into mold. Place in refrigerator and let stand about 2 hours longer.

Topping

Makes enough for 2 molds

    1 cup sour cream
    1 package (8 ounces) cream cheese
   ½ cup sugar
   ½ teaspoon vanilla extract
      Nuts (optional)

Combine first 4 ingredients and mix well at room temperature. Store in refrigerator. Add topping just before serving. Top with nuts, if desired.

Fresh-Is Best-Vegetable Salad

Makes 4 servings

    1 envelope Knox® Unflavored Gelatine
    2 tablespoons sugar
    1 cup boiling water
    1 cup (8 ounces) plain yogurt
    1 tablespoon white or cider vinegar
    1 to 2 tablespoons finely chopped green onion
   ½ teaspoon dill weed
      Vegetable combinations (suggestions follow)

In a medium bowl, mix Knox Unflavored Gelatine with sugar. Add boiling water and stir until gelatine is completely dissolved. Blend in yogurt, vinegar, green onions, and dill weed. Chill, stirring occasionally, until mixture is the consistency of unbeaten egg whites. Fold in desired vegetable combination. Turn into individual molds or a 3-cup mold; chill until firm. Unmold to serve.

Vegetable combinations: Choose 1 cup shredded cucumber and ½ cup shredded radish; or ½ cup *each* chopped cauliflower, green pepper, and tomato; or ½ cup *each* chopped tomato, fresh mushrooms, and cooked fresh green beans.

Tri-Color Vegetable Mold

Makes 10 servings

    3 cups boiling water
    3 packages (3 ounces each) lemon-flavored gelatin
    2 cups cold water
   ¼ cup white vinegar
 1¼ teaspoons salt
    2 cups shredded carrots
    2 cups Hellmann's or Best Foods Real Mayon-
      naise
 1½ cups chopped cabbage
    2 cups coarsely chopped fresh spinach
    1 teaspoon grated onion

In medium bowl, pour boiling water over gelatin; stir until dissolved. Stir in cold water, vinegar, and salt. Measure 1¾ cups into small bowl; set remaining gelatin aside. Place bowl in larger bowl of ice and water. Stir gelatin until mixture is uniformly thickened. Fold in carrots; spoon into 8-cup mold or 9-inch loaf pan; chill until set but not firm. Meanwhile, measure 1½ cups of gelatin into small bowl. With mixer or wire whisk, beat in mayonnaise until smooth. Stir over ice until mixture is uniformly thickened. Fold in cabbage; spoon over carrot layer. Chill until set but not firm. Meanwhile, stir remaining gelatin over ice until mixture is uniformly thickened. Fold in spinach and onion; spoon over cabbage layer. Chill at least 4 hours, or until firm. Unmold.

Crunchy Vegetable Pop-Ups

Makes 9 to 12 servings

    1 can (3 to 4 ounces) chopped mushrooms
    2 envelopes Knox⊚ Unflavored Gelatine
    2 cups boiling water
    4 teaspoons sugar
    1 teaspoon salt
   ¾ cup lemon juice
   ½ cup *each* finely chopped green pepper, cucum-
      ber, and radishes
    1 cup *each* finely chopped cauliflower and celery
      Lettuce leaves

Drain mushrooms, reserving liquid. To reserved liquid add enough water to make ½ cup. In a medium bowl, mix liquid with Knox Unflavored Gelatine. Add boiling water and stir until gelatine is completely dissolved. Stir in sugar, salt, and lemon juice. Chill, stirring occasionally, until mixture is the consistency of unbeaten egg whites. Fold in mushrooms and fresh vegetables. Turn into 2 sectioned ice-cube trays; chill until firm. Unmold; serve 3 or 4 cubes on individual lettuce-lined salad plates.

Molding How-Tos

Gelatin salads look their most spectacular when molded. The making and the unmolding can be simple, if you follow these molding tips.

Use less water in preparing the gelatin mixture if salad is to be molded. For 3-ounce package of gelatin, use ¾ cup cold water; for 6-ounce package, use 1½ cups cold water. This makes the mold less fragile and makes unmolding much simpler.

As for the mold itself, almost any metal form, not necessarily the traditional mold, will work. If you have a collection of molds, that's fine. But if you lack them, consider using any of these less usual pans for molding. Use cake pans—square 8- or 9-inch pans, round pans, fluted tube pans, tube pans, or loaf cake or bread pans. Use metal mixing bowls; the nested sets give you a variety of sizes. Or use metal cans, from fruits or juices; to unmold, dip can in warm water, then puncture bottom of can and unmold.

Determine the volume of the mold first by measuring with water. Most recipes give an indication of the size mold needed. For clear gelatin, figure a 3-ounce package will make a little less than 2 cups, a 6-ounce package makes less than 4 cups. If mold holds less than the amount called for, the surplus might be poured into a separate dish for serving later. If the mold is much too big for the amount of gelatin mixture, it will be difficult to unmold and either the recipe should be increased or a smaller mold should be used.

To arrange fruits or vegetables in molds, spoon enough of the liquid gelatin into the bottom of the mold to form a thin layer. Chill until set, either by placing it in the refrigerator or by setting it into a bed of cracked ice. Then arrange a design made up of cut vegetables, fruit, meat, etc., on the just-set gelatin, spoon another thin layer of gelatin over it and chill it again until it is firm. Continue by following recipe directions.

Now, the unmolding. First allow gelatin to set until firm, several hours or overnight. Also, chill serving plate or individual plates on which mold will be served.

- Make certain that gelatin is completely firm. It should not feel sticky on top and should not sag toward the side if mold is tilted.

- Use a small pointed knife dipped in warm water to loosen top edge. Or, moisten tips of fingers and gently pull gelatin from edge of mold.

- Dip mold in warm, not hot, water, just to the rim, for about 10 seconds. Lift from water, hold upright, and shake slightly to loosen gelatin. Or, gently pull gelatin from edge of mold.

- Moisten top of gelatin and the chilled serving plate with cold water; this allows gelatin to be moved after unmolding. Place moistened plate over mold and invert. Shake slightly, then lift off mold carefully If gelatin doesn't release easily, dip the mold in warm water again. If necessary, move gelatin to center of serving plate.

What Goes with What?

Almost any food you can think of combines beautifully with unflavored gelatin. Here are some ideas to get you started.

Liquid: Fresh, frozen, or canned fruit juice. Fruit punches, nectars, and ades. Tomato and other vegetable juices or combinations. Broths.

Fruits: Fresh, frozen, or canned peaches, plums, pears, apricots, grapes, cherries. All varieties of berries and melons. Canned pineapple, fruit cocktail.

Vegetables, raw: Finely shredded green or red cabbage, spinach, or carrots. Chopped celery, green pepper, cucumber, or cauliflower. Sliced green onions or radishes.

Vegetables, cooked: Canned, frozen, or cooked fresh cut green or wax beans, corn, asparagus, lima beans, sliced carrots, peas, kidney beans, chick-peas (garbanzos).

Meat, poultry, fish, shellfish: Diced cooked chicken, ham, tongue, pork, veal, beef. Flaked cooked fish of any kind. Flaked canned tuna, salmon. Flaked crab meat. Diced shrimp or lobster.

That's not the end of course, only the beginning. Virtually anything you like to eat will combine with unflavored gelatin into an exciting new-way dish. Here are some anything-goes-with-anything combinations for you to try. Then use your inventiveness to go on from there with new combinations.

Salads: Clear gel with cabbage, carrots, green onions, radishes. Tomato juice gel with tuna or shrimp, cucumber, green onions, olives. Beef broth gel with ham or beef, lima beans, cauliflower, radishes, green pepper. Chicken broth gel with chicken or veal, celery, pimiento, onion.

Desserts: Orange gel with peaches and strawberries. Lemon gel with fruit cocktail. Cranberry-juice gel with oranges and walnuts. Fruit-punch gel with pears and grapes. Apricot gel with melon balls and blueberries.

Pasta and Rice with Pizzazz

Here's how to turn old-fashioned standbys like macaroni and rice into dishes as up-to-date as the trendiest new restaurant.

Light Tuna and Shells

Makes 4 to 6 servings

2½ cups (8 ounces) San Giorgio® Shell Macaroni, uncooked
1 can (6½ or 7 ounces) water-packed tuna, drained and flaked
1 cup thinly sliced celery
½ cup sliced carrots
½ cup sliced sweet pickles
¼ cup finely chopped onion
1 cup (8-ounce bottle) creamy cucumber reduced-calorie dressing
Salt and pepper to taste

Cook shell macaroni according to package directions; drain. Cool. (Rinse with cold water to cool quickly; drain well.) Combine cooled shell macaroni with remaining ingredients and toss lightly. Chill.

Buttons 'n' Bows Noodle Salad

Makes about 4 servings

1 package (8 ounces) egg noodle bows
¾ cup Wish-Bone® Thousand Island Dressing
1 cup thinly sliced celery
½ cup sliced pimiento-stuffed olives
¼ cup finely chopped onion
1 hard-cooked egg, chopped

Cook noodles according to package directions; drain and rinse with cold water until completely cool. In large bowl, combine Wish-Bone Thousand Island Dressing, noodles, celery, olives, onion, and egg; chill.

Light Rotini Luncheon Salad

Makes about 6 servings

3 cups (8 ounces) San Giorgio® Rotini, uncooked
2 cups cubed cooked chicken
2 cups cherry tomatoes, halved
2 cups thinly sliced green pepper strips
2 cups fresh raw broccoli flowerets
1 cup (8-ounce bottle) zesty Italian reduced-calorie dressing
Salt and pepper to taste

Cook rotini according to package directions; drain. Cool. (Rinse with cold water to cool quickly; drain well.) Combine cooled rotini with remaining ingredients and toss lightly. Chill.

Macaroni-Vegetable Salad

Makes 10 to 12 servings

2 cups uncooked elbow macaroni
1 package (10 ounces) frozen mixed vegetables, cooked and drained
1 cup chopped celery
⅓ cup chopped radishes
Salt and pepper to taste
¾ cup Wish-Bone® Creamy Cucumber Dressing

Cook macaroni according to package directions; drain. In large bowl, combine all ingredients except dressing. Chill thoroughly. Add Wish-Bone Creamy Cucumber Dressing and toss gently before serving.

Light Rotini Luncheon Salad; Light Tuna and Shells. HERSHEY Pasta Group

Irish Mac Salad

Makes 6 servings

    1 can (12 ounces) Armour Star Corned Beef,
        shredded
    2 cups cooked elbow macaroni
    1 cup sour cream
    ¼ cup chopped green pepper
    ¼ cup chopped celery
    2 tablespoons chopped onion
    1 teaspoon salt
    1 teaspoon prepared mustard
    ¼ teaspoon pepper
      Lettuce cups

Combine all ingredients except lettuce cups; chill thoroughly. Serve in lettuce cups.

Sensational Ham-Noodle Salad

Makes 4 to 6 servings

    1 package (8 ounces) enriched egg noodles
    ½ cup Wish-Bone® Deluxe French or Creamy
        Cucumber Dressing
    ¼ cup sour cream
    1 cup diced cooked ham
    1 cup diced cheddar cheese
    ½ cup diced green pepper
    ¼ cup sliced radishes
    2 tablespoons sweet pickle relish
    1 tablespoon lemon juice

Cook noodles according to package directions; drain and rinse in cold water until completely cool. In large bowl, thoroughly combine deluxe French dressing and sour cream. Add noodles, ham, cheese, green pepper, radishes, relish, and lemon juice; toss lightly and chill.

Chicken Pasta Salad

Makes 4 servings

    ¼ cup Mazola Corn Oil
    ¼ cup sliced green onions
    3 tablespoons white wine vinegar
    1 teaspoon grated orange rind
    2 tablespoons orange juice
    ½ teaspoon dry mustard
    ¼ teaspoon salt
    ¹⁄₁₆ teaspoon ground red pepper
    2 cups cooked chicken strips or cubes
    6 ounces Mueller's Linguine or Spaghetti, broken,
        cooked, drained, and cooled.
    ¼ pound snow peas, trimmed (1 cup)
    1 cup orange sections
      Lettuce leaves (optional)
    2 tablespoons slivered almonds, toasted

In large bowl, stir together corn oil, green onions, vinegar, orange rind and juice, mustard, and pepper. Add chicken and linguine; toss to coat well. Cover; refrigerate about 2 hours. Just before serving, add snow peas and oranges; toss lightly. If desired, spoon into lettuce-lined serving bowl. Sprinkle with almonds.

Tuna-and-Radish Macaroni Salad

Makes 6 servings

    3 cups cooked elbow macaroni
    2 tomatoes, cubed (about 2½ cups)
    1 can (7 ounces) tuna, drained and flaked
    1 cup sliced celery
    ½ cup sliced radishes
    ½ cup Mazola Corn Oil
    ¼ cup white vinegar
    1 clove garlic, minced or pressed
    1 teaspoon salt
    ¼ teaspoon oregano
    ¼ teaspoon pepper
      Lettuce leaves

In large bowl, toss together macaroni, tomatoes, tuna, celery, and radishes. In small bowl, stir together oil, vinegar, garlic, salt, oregano, and pepper until well blended. Pour over macaroni mixture; toss to coat well. Cover; refrigerate several hours to blend flavors. Serve in lettuce-lined bowl.

Smackaroni Salad

Makes 6 servings

    1 package (4 ounces) Armour Star Hard Salami,
        cut in julienne strips
    2 cups cooked shell macaroni
    1 cup chopped celery
    1 cup cherry tomato halves
    1 cup whole pitted ripe olives
    ½ cup finely chopped green pepper
    ¼ cup finely chopped green onions
    ½ cup Italian salad dressing
    1 teaspoon salt

Combine all ingredients; toss lightly. Chill.

Make Now, Toss Later

To achieve optimum eye appeal for your mixed green salad, prepare your choice of greens and combine them in the salad bowl. (A shallow wide bowl is better than a deep narrow one—it shows off your pretty salad better and, when the salad is tossed, all the delightful surprises you've added don't sink to the bottom and get lost.) Cover the salad and refrigerate it until just before you're ready to serve. Then arrange on top of the bed of greens whatever garnish you're going to add—for flavor, for texture, for substance, or just for pretty—in an attractive pattern. Bring the salad and its dressing to the table separately and then, when everyone's eye is pleased and appetite whetted, dress, toss, and serve it immediately. Besides the bonus of beauty, you'll achieve maximum crispness this way—a great virtue in the taste of a salad.

What can you use to make the attractively arranged garnish? Almost anything that leaps to your mind. Try these, separately or in any number of combinations, to get you started:

- cubes or slivers of cheese (any kind)
- small pretzel sticks or crumbled larger pretzels
- plain or flavored croutons, packaged or homemade
- sliced raw mushrooms
- shredded carrots, or a mound of carrot curls
- sliced or shredded white or red radishes
- bite-size dry cereal
- nuts (any kind), plain, salted, or toasted
- coarsely crumbled corn chips or potato chips
- canned (drained) kidney beans, white beans, or chick-peas
- paper-thin strips of turnip, rutabaga, or beet
- crumbled crisp bacon
- meat or poultry (any kind) in chunks or strips
- packaged stuffing mix
- canned or packaged Chinese noodles
- rings of sweet white or red onion
- broken cheese crackers
- paper-thin rings of sweet red or green pepper
- sliced water chestnuts
- packaged coconut chips
- pickle slices or chunks
- whole or halved grapes
- avocado slices or chunks
- canned French-fried onions
- pimiento slivers
- tomato slices, chunks, or halved cherry tomatoes
- chopped or sliced hard-cooked egg
- plain or seasoned popcorn
- orange or grapefruit sections
- sliced bamboo shoots

Raisin Rice al Fresco

Makes 4 to 6 servings

- 2 cups water
- 1 teaspoon salt
- ¼ teaspoon thyme
- ⅛ teaspoon saffron
- 1 bay leaf
- ½ cup long-grained rice
- ⅓ cup vegetable oil
- 3 tablespoons red wine vinegar
- ¼ teaspoon coarsely cracked pepper
- ½ cup minced green pepper
- ½ cup minced red onion
- ⅓ cup Sun-Maid® Seedless Raisins
- 1 small tomato, coarsely chopped
- ¼ cup chopped parsley

Bring the water to a boil with the salt, thyme, saffron, and bay leaf. Stir in the rice and return to a boil. Reduce heat, cover, and simmer for 20 minutes. Meanwhile, combine the oil, vinegar, and cracked pepper to form a dressing. Drain the cooked rice and turn it into a bowl. Remove the bay leaf. Add the dressing and toss well with a fork. Allow the rice to stand for 10 minutes, giving it an occasional toss. Add the remaining ingredients and toss with a fork until well blended. Chill well before serving.

Currant-Brown Rice Salad

Makes 4 to 6 servings

- 2 cups cooked brown rice
- ½ cup Sun-Maid® Zante Currants
- ½ cup coarsely chopped walnuts
- 4 scallions, sliced
- ¼ cup chopped parsley
- ¼ cup olive oil
- 3 tablespoons white wine vinegar or lemon juice
- 1 tablespoon Dijon-style mustard
- 1 small clove garlic, minced
- ½ teaspoon thyme
- ¾ teaspoon salt
- ⅛ teaspoon freshly ground pepper
  Lettuce leaves
  Additional chopped parsley

In a large bowl, toss the rice with the currants, walnuts, scallions, and parsley. Combine the remaining ingredients except lettuce and additional chopped parsley in a small bowl and beat with a fork until well blended; pour over the rice salad, tossing lightly. Cover and refrigerate for several hours; toss occasionally. Serve the salad in a lettuce-lined bowl, sprinkled with chopped parsley.

Simply Successful Rice Salad

Makes 8 to 10 servings

 2 **Boil-in-bags Success Rice**
 ½ **cup finely chopped onion**
 ½ **cup finely chopped green pepper**
 ½ **cup sweet pickle relish**
 ¼ **cup diced pimiento**
 ¼ **cup sliced ripe olives**
 4 **hard-cooked eggs, chopped**
 ¾ **cup mayonnaise**
 2 **teaspoons prepared mustard**
 1 **teaspoon salt**
 ½ **teaspoon ground black pepper**
    Lettuce
    Tomato wedges, ripe olives, egg slices
       (optional)

Prepare rice according to package directions. Cool. Add onion, green pepper, relish, pimiento, olives, and eggs. Combine remaining ingredients and stir into rice mixture until thoroughly blended. Chill. Serve on bed of lettuce and garnish with tomato wedges, ripe olives, and egg slices, if desired.

> **Q.** *We like stuffed tomato salads, but juice always leaks out of the tomato and makes the salad watery. What should I do?*
>
> **A.** Prepare the tomatoes in advance. Skin them or not as you prefer; with a sharp knife, cut out a portion of the interior from the stem end. Salt the tomatoes lightly and turn them upside down on several thicknesses of paper towel to drain. Put the salad filling into the tomatoes just before you serve them.

Simply Successful Rice Salad. Riviana Foods Inc.

Brown Rice Salad (page 100). Courtesy of The J.M. Smucker Co.

Brown Rice Salad

Makes 6 to 8 servings
 2½ cups water
  1 cup brown rice
 ¾ cup Smucker's Grape Jelly
 ½ cup fresh lemon juice
 ¼ cup olive oil
  2 tablespoons dried mint leaves
 ½ teaspoon salt
  1 cup chopped parsley
  2 cucumbers, peeled, halved, seeded, and diced
  1 cup chopped red radishes
 ½ cup chopped green onions
    Large lettuce leaves (optional)

In medium saucepan, bring water to a boil. Add rice. Cover and cook over low heat about 45 minutes, or until water is absorbed and rice is tender. Cool. In blender container, combine grape jelly, lemon juice, oil, mint, and salt. Cover and blend until smooth. In straight-sided 1½-quart glass bowl or soufflé dish, place rice in layer; add layer of parsley, half of cucumbers. Pour half of dressing over layers. Add radishes and remaining cucumbers, topping with onions. Add remaining dressing and refrigerate several hours or overnight. Toss before serving. For easy eating, spoon salad onto large lettuce leaf, roll up and eat out of hand.

Bulgur Salad

For a bulgur salad, omit brown rice. Cook 1 cup bulgur in 2 cups boiling water until tender, about 15 minutes.

Spinach Rice Salad

Makes 6 to 8 servings
  1 cup Uncle Ben's® Converted® Brand Rice
 ½ cup bottled Italian salad dressing
  1 tablespoon soy sauce
 ½ teaspoon sugar
  2 cups fresh spinach, cut into thin strips
 ½ cup sliced celery
 ½ cup sliced green onions, including tops
 ⅓ cup crumbled crisp bacon

Cook rice according to package directions. Cool slightly. Combine dressing, soy sauce, and sugar. Stir into warm rice. Cover and chill. Fold in remaining ingredients before serving.

Cool-as-a-Cucumber Kasha Salad

Makes 6 to 7 servings
  3 cups cold cooked kasha
  5 to 6 sliced fresh mushrooms
 ½ cup sliced scallions
  1 medium cucumber, seeded and diced
 ½ cup sliced celery
  1 medium tomato, seeded and diced
  2 cups cooled cooked peas
 ¼ cup chopped parsley
 ½ cup sliced green or black olives
 ½ cup sliced water chestnuts (optional)
  1 bottle (8 ounces) French dressing or mayonnaise, or oil and vinegar

Toss all ingredients with dressing. Chill at least 2 hours before serving.

Raisin Tabouli

Makes 4 servings
 ½ cup Sun-Maid® Seedless Raisins
 ½ cup bulgur
 ⅔ cup boiling water
 ½ cup olive oil
 ⅓ cup lemon juice
  1 tablespoon chopped fresh mint or 1 teaspoon dried mint
 ¼ teaspoon dill weed
  1 teaspoon salt
 ½ teaspoon freshly ground pepper
 1½ cups sliced mushrooms
  1 cup finely chopped parsley
  1 cup thinly sliced scallions
    Lettuce leaves
    Tomato wedges

Combine the raisins with the bulgur and add the boiling water. Let stand for 30 minutes, then drain off any excess water. Combine the oil with the lemon juice, mint, dill weed, salt, and pepper and toss with the bulgur. Toss in the mushrooms, parsley, and scallions. Cover and chill, tossing occasionally. Serve in a lettuce-lined bowl with tomato wedges.

Salad Oils

If you are old enough—and that's quite old—you may remember cod liver or halibut liver oil, rich in vitamins A and D, being given you (given is too mild a word—poured down your throat is better) when you were a child; it had a taste so incredibly awful that once experienced it cannot be entirely put out of mind by the passing years. There are other animal oils, too—whale oil, for lamps, is an example. But the oils we use in foods are all mild vegetable products, removed from plant materials by pressing or melting.

To be technical about it, oil is a substance of viscous (slippery/sticky) texture, fluid at room temperature, insoluble in water. In the kitchen we use oil for rich texture and/or flavor, as in salad dressings; a cooking medium, as in sautéing, shallow or deep-fat frying; shortening, the tenderizer in cakes, pastries, quick breads. Such edible oils, common in American kitchens, are obtained from corn, cottonseed, olives and soybeans, among other plants. And there are many more. Some come readily to hand, others fall under the heading of culinary exotica.

Here are a few of the better-known edible oils used around the world.

Almond oil: Faintly sweet, used in the making of confectionery of many kinds; it is the "essential oil" from which almond flavoring extract is made.

Coconut oil: Used in Africa and southeast Asia for cooking; here, we are more likely to encounter it in cosmetic products, such as soaps and shampoos.

Corn oil: This in one of our most commonly used cooking oils; it is completely tasteless. Because it does not smoke at usual frying temperatures, it is excellent for deep-fat frying.

Cottonseed oil: As a straight cooking oil, this is used mostly by East Indians; it is a component of a number of our vegetable shortenings and some margarines.

Grape-seed oil: Not widely available here, it it a fine salad oil, with excellent odor and flavor.

Mustard-seed oil: Also much used in East Indian cookery, this has a strong mustardy flavor; Italy uses it to flavor those delightful mustard-syrup pickled fruits, *mostarda di frutta.*

Olive oil: We are grateful to Italian immigrants who brought the use of olive oil to this country; delicate but distinctive of flavor, this is a fine salad oil and is essential to the many dishes we learned how to prepare from our Italian neighbors and have made a part of the glorious mishmash that is American cooking. Olive oil labeled "virgin" is from the first pressing and is light and delicate of flavor.

Peanut (also called groundnut) oil: Another that is often used in American kitchens, more often in French ones. Once it had a pleasant, mild peanut flavor (the kind used in southeast Asia still does) but nowadays is refined so as to be tasteless.

Rape (also called colza) oil: The second most widely used oil of the Mediterranean area, it is seldom available here.

Safflower oil: Made from the seeds of the false saffron, native to Asia but now grown here; light and virtually tasteless (there is a slightly nutty overtone), the oil has found a place in American kitchens since the time, a number of years ago, when its use was urged in a diet book that became a best seller. (Don't be misled into thinking it is lower in calories than other oils. It is not; its "low" is saturated fat, also true of corn and some other kitchen oils, all of them useful on low-cholesterol diets.)

Sesame seed oil: This one is flavorful, with a rich and robust, somewhat nutlike taste. Prized in Oriental cookery, it often is used as a flavoring or to mask strong fish flavors.

Sunflower oil: Light, with a mildy nutlike flavor, this is neither widely available nor widely used in American kitchens.

Walnut oil: The salad-dressing oil of choice for French cooks; except in the walnut-growing areas of France it is so expensive that it is usually hoarded for special-occasion salads.

Buying and Using Oil

Unless you use a good deal of oil in your kitchen, don't buy in large amounts. Although it keeps relatively well, oil does eventually get rancid—that is, it decomposes and acquires an unpleasant odor and flavor. Although this may not occur for 2 or 3 months, rancidity may develop sooner if the oil is exposed to moisture or light; it can also pick up, undesirably, the flavors of other foods if not kept tightly covered. Store in a kitchen shelf, in cool darkness. If you must for some reason store oil for a long period, put it—again, tightly covered—in the refrigerator; it will become cloudy and thicker than it originally was, but be usable. The exception to this is olive oil, which will solidify at refrigerator temperatures over a long period.

Pure oil is pure fat—it contains no other nutrients. A tablespoon of oil furnishes in the neighborhood of 120 calories, a cup slightly under 2,000.

Centerpiece Salads

*Make-a-meal salads are the no-fuss—deliciously fresh—
solutions for lunches and light dinners.*

Golden Gate Beef Salad

Makes 4 servings

- ¼ cup lemon juice
- 1 cup water
- ⅓ cup sugar
- 1 tablespoon oil
- 1¼ teaspoons salt
- 1 clove garlic, minced
- ½ teaspoon ground ginger
- ¼ teaspoon anise seed
- ⅛ teaspoon ground cinnamon
- ⅛ teaspoon cloves
- 1 pound cooked beef, cut in thin strips
- 2 cups cauliflowerets, blanched 3 minutes
- 1 package (6 ounces) frozen pea pods, thawed
- 1 red onion, thinly sliced
- 2 oranges
- ½ pound spinach

Combine lemon juice, water, sugar, oil, salt, garlic, ginger, anise seed, cinnamon, and cloves in small saucepan; simmer 10 minutes. Cool. Place beef strips in utility dish or plastic bag. Pour ½ marinade mixture over meat, turning to coat. Cover dish or tie bag securely; marinate in refrigerator 4 hours or overnight. Place cauliflowerets, pea pods, and onion in utility dish or plastic bag; pour remainder of marinade over vegetables. Cover dish or tie bag securely; marinate in refrigerator 3 to 4 hours. Pare oranges, removing rind and white membrane. Cut on both sides of separating membrane to remove sections. Add orange sections to vegetables in marinade, tossing to coat; remove from marinade. Place spinach leaves on platter and drizzle vegetable marinade over leaves. Arrange vegetables and orange sections over spinach. Remove meat from marinade and arrange on top of vegetables.

Jellied Meat Salad

Makes 4 servings

- 2 tablespoons cold water
- 1 tablespoon lemon juice
- 1 envelope unflavored gelatin
- ⅔ cup boiling water
- 2 beef or chicken bouillon cubes
- 1 stalk celery, cut up
- 1 small carrot, pared and cut up
- ¼ medium green pepper, seeded and cut up
- 1 thin slice onion
- 1 cup cubed cooked lean meat or poultry
- 1 cup cracked or crushed ice
- Salad greens

Put cold water and lemon juice into blender container. Sprinkle on gelatin; let stand 1 minute. Add boiling water and bouillon cubes. Cover; blend at low speed until gelatin and bouillon cubes are dissolved. Add remaining ingredients except salad greens to blender container in order listed. Cover; blend at medium speed just until vegetables and meat are chopped. If necessary, stop blender during processing and push ingredients toward blades with rubber spatula. Pour into 3-cup mold or 4 individual molds. Chill until set. Unmold onto salad greens.

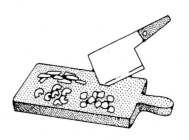

Hawaiian Salad (page 104). Armour Food Company

Hot Taco Salad

Makes 4 sevings

    1 pound lean ground beef
    1 can (16 ounces) stewed tomatoes
    1 can (4 ounces) chopped green chilies, drained
    2 teaspoons Wyler's® Beef-Flavor Instant Bouillon
        or 2 Beef-Flavor Bouillon Cubes
    ½ teaspoon hot pepper sauce
    ⅛ teaspoon garlic powder
       Dash pepper
    1 quart shredded lettuce (1 medium head)
    1 to 1½ cups corn chips
    1 medium tomato, chopped (about 1 cup)
    1 cup (4 ounces) shredded cheddar cheese

In large skillet, brown meat; pour off fat. Add remaining ingredients except lettuce, corn chips, chopped tomato, and cheese. Simmer uncovered 30 minutes. In large bowl or platter, arrange all ingredients; toss to serve.

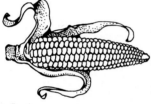

Hawaiian Salad

Makes 4 to 6 servings

    1 cup Armour Star Spiced Luncheon Meat, cut in
        julienne strips
    2 cups shredded cabbage
    1 cup shredded lettuce
    1 cup chopped celery
    1 can (20 ounces) pineapple chunks, drained
    ¼ cup chopped green pepper
    1 tablespoon vinegar
    1 teaspoon prepared horseradish

Combine all ingredients; toss lightly. Chill thoroughly.

Ham-Pineapple Petal Salad

Makes 2 servings

    1 can (6¾ ounces) Hormel Chunk Ham, flaked
    ¼ cup chopped green pepper
    2 tablespoons chopped celery
    2 teaspoons chopped stuffed green olives
    ¼ cup mayonnaise
       Lettuce leaves
    4 canned pineapple slices, drained and chilled
       Additional stuffed green olives

Combine ham, green pepper, celery, olives, and mayonnaise. Cover and chill until serving time. Arrange lettuce leaves on 2 salad plates. Halve pineapple slices; place 4 halves on each plate to form a scalloped edge. Mound ham mixture in center. Garnish with additional olives, if desired.

Low-Cal Chef's Salad

Makes 4 servings

    1½ quarts mixed salad greens, rinsed and torn into
        bite-size pieces
    ½ cup chopped green onions
    ½ cup sliced radishes
    ¼ pound thinly sliced cooked chicken (white
        meat), cut into strips
    ¼ pound thinly sliced boiled ham, cut into strips
    6 slices Borden® Lite-Line® Pasteurized Process
        Cheese Product, cut into strips
    1 medium tomato, cut into wedges
    1 medium hard-cooked egg, sliced
    6 tablespoons bottled low-calorie Italian dressing

In large bowl, toss greens, onions, and radishes. Arrange on large platter; top with remaining ingredients except dressing. Serve with dressing.

Garnishing Salads

Most salads are, by their very nature, good to look at. Salad ingredients are beautiful in themselves. The greens alone range in color from pale tender to dark assertive, in shape from smooth flat to stand-up curly, in size from minute to plate-covering, in texture from buttery to crisp, in flavor from bland to bitey.

There are many other possible green additions to a tossed salad that can add zest, texture and flavor contrast, and—never forget it—beauty. Long, thin slivers of scallion, including some of the tops. All the cabbages—young and tender new cabbage, crinkly savoy, pale and mild nappa. Celery and fennel slices. Artichoke hearts (frozen, cooked, or from cans or jars). Bean sprouts and alfalfa sprouts. Snipped chives. Thin rounds or spears of cucumber and zucchini. Fresh-from-the-garden (yours or the greengrocer's) herbs, such as dill, basil, tarragon, mint, chervil, coriander, and summer savory.

Dilly of a Deli Salad

Makes about 6 servings
- ⅓ cup Wish-Bone® Italian Dressing
- ¾ cup mayonnaise
- 4 cups thinly sliced cooked potatoes or 3 cans (16 ounces each) sliced potatoes, drained
- ¾ pound cold meats, cut into ½-inch cubes (suggestions follow)
- ½ pound assorted cheeses, shredded (suggestions follow)
- 1 medium tomato, coarsely chopped and drained
- ½ cup chopped dill pickle spears
  Additional dill pickle spears (optional)

In large bowl, blend Italian dressing with mayonnaise; add potatoes, cold meats, cheeses, tomato, and pickles and toss until coated. Pack into an 8-inch springform pan and chill 4 hours or overnight. Garnish, if desired, with dill pickle spears.

Suggested cold meats: Use any combination of the following: salami, ham, turkey, corned beef, roast beef, bologna, or your favorite cold meats.

Suggested cheeses: Use any combination of the following: American, cheddar, Swiss, Muenster, brick, or your favorite cheeses.

Ham Waldorf Salad

Makes 3 to 4 servings
- 2 medium apples, quartered, cored, and cubed
- 1 tablespoon lemon juice
- 1 cup cubed Armour Star Chopped Ham
- ¼ cup sliced celery
- ¼ cup mayonnaise
- 2 tablespoons chopped walnuts

In large bowl, toss apples with lemon juice. Add remaining ingredients; mix well. Chill.

Salami Bean Salad

Makes about 1½ cups salad
- ½ cup Vienna® pure beef salami, diced
- ⅓ cup cooked cut green beans
- ⅓ cup cooked cut wax beans
- ⅓ cup canned kidney beans, drained
- 1 teaspoon chopped green pepper
- 1 teaspoon chopped onion
- 2 tablespoons vinegar
- 1 tablespoon salad oil
- ½ teaspoon sugar

Combine all ingredients and mix well. May be made ahead and stored in refrigerator to marinate overnight.

Aloha Salad

Makes 6 servings
- 1 cup long-grain rice
- 1 can (20 ounces) pineapple chunks
- 2 cans (6¾ ounces each) Hormel Chunk Ham, drained and coarsely chopped
- ⅔ cup thinly sliced celery
- ⅓ cup chopped green pepper
- ⅔ cup mayonnaise
- 2 tablespoons honey
- 1 tablespoon lemon juice
- ⅛ teaspoon ground ginger
  Lettuce leaves

Cook rice according to package directions. Cool slightly; pack into well-oiled 4-cup ring mold. Cool to room temperature; chill. Drain pineapple, reserving 1 tablespoon syrup. Combine ham, pineapple chunks, celery, and green pepper; chill. Before serving, mix mayonnaise, honey, lemon juice, ginger, and reserved tablespoon pineapple syrup. Pour ½ cup dressing over ham mixture; mix gently. Unmold rice onto lettuce-lined serving plate. Spoon ham mixture into center of ring. Serve with remaining dressing.

Ham, Sweet Potato, and Orange Cranberry Salad

Makes 6 servings
- 3 large sweet potatoes
- 3 navel oranges
- 2 cups thinly sliced celery
- 3 cups diced smoked ham
- 1 can (8 ounces) Ocean Spray Jellied Cranberry Sauce, cut into ½-inch cubes
  Lettuce leaves
- ½ cup vegetable oil
- ½ cup orange juice
- 2 teaspoons sugar
- 1 teaspoon salt
- ¼ teaspoon pepper

Cover sweet potatoes with water in a large saucepan. Bring to boil and cook until they can be easily pierced with fork. Drain and cool. Peel and cut into ½-inch cubes. Set aside. Peel and section oranges. In a mixing bowl, combine potatoes, oranges, celery, ham, and jellied cranberry sauce. Toss gently to mix. Line a serving bowl with lettuce leaves; spoon in potato mixture. Cover and chill. In a mixing bowl, beat oil, orange juice, sugar, salt, and pepper until thick and well blended. Let stand at room temperature for 1 hour. Beat again to blend and pour over salad. Serve at once.

Swiss Salami Salad

Makes 4 servings

    1 package (4 ounces) Armour Star Hard Salami,
        sliced in thin strips
    1 cup (4 ounces) shredded Swiss cheese
    ¼ cup chopped green pepper
    ¼ cup chopped celery
    2 tablespoons chopped green onion
    ⅓ cup mayonnaise
    1 cup croutons
      Lettuce cups
      Grated Parmesan cheese

Combine salami, Swiss cheese, green pepper, celery, onions, and mayonnaise; chill. Just before serving, add croutons; toss lightly. Serve in lettuce cups; sprinkle with Parmesan cheese.

Cantaloupe-SPAM® Salad

Makes 4 servings

      Lettuce leaves
    1 can (12 ounces) SPAM®, cut in
        chunks
    1 medium cantaloupe, seeded, peeled, and cut in
        chunks
    1 small green pepper, seeded and chopped
    1 can (8 ounces) crushed pineapple, drained
    3 tablespoons sour cream
    3 tablespoons yogurt
    ¼ teaspoon sugar

Place lettuce leaves on salad plates; mound SPAM® in center. Surround with cantaloupe. Sprinkle green pepper over top. Combine pineapple, sour cream, yogurt, and sugar; pour over salad.

Q. *I have recently moved from the East to the West Coast. All the mushrooms here look old. I'm used to those nice white mushrooms back home. Here they're brown and sort of shaggy looking. What's wrong with them?*
A. Nothing's wrong. They're simply a different kind of mushroom. The Western variety does need a rather more careful scrutiny when you buy them, to make sure they're good. The brown mushrooms—golden cream is their name, but it doesn't describe them very well—are a newer variety. However, Western markets do carry the familiar white mushrooms in small containers, like berry boxes. If you don't take to the brown ones, buy the white—there is little if any difference in price.

Pizza Heart (page 108). Ocean Spray Cranberries

Hearty Franks 'n' Beer Salad

Makes 4 to 6 servings

    ¾ cup Wish-Bone® Italian Dressing
    ¾ cup beer
    ½ teaspoon caraway seed
    1 tablespoon brown sugar
    1 pound frankfurters or knockwurst, cooked and
        sliced diagonally
    4 cups thinly sliced cooked potatoes
    1 red onion, cut into rings
    2 quarts mixed salad greens, rinsed and torn into
        bite-size pieces
      Cherry tomatoes (optional)

In large shallow baking dish, blend Wish-Bone Italian Dressing, beer, caraway seed, and brown sugar; add frankfurters, potatoes, and onion. Cover and marinate in refrigerator, turning occasionally, at least 3 hours. To serve, arrange marinated mixture on salad greens; toss with marinade. Garnish, if desired, with cherry tomatoes.

Turkey-Fruit Toss (page 113). Armour Food Company

Festive Salad

Makes 6 servings

   2 pounds potatoes (6 medium)
   ⅓ cup mayonnaise
   ⅓ cup sour cream
   ½ cup chopped celery
   ⅓ cup chopped onion
   ¼ cup chopped green pepper
   1 tablespoon milk
   ½ teaspoon salt
      Pepper to taste
   1 can (12 ounces) SPAM®, diced, divided
   1 cup halved cherry tomatoes
      Green pepper rings
      Radishes, coarsely chopped

Cook potatoes in boiling salted water until tender; drain. Cool slightly; peel. When cooled to room temperature, slice thin. In medium bowl, combine mayonnaise, sour cream, celery, onion, green pepper, milk, salt, and pepper; gently stir in potatoes. In 2-quart serving dish, spread one-quarter of the potato salad over bottom; sprinkle with half of SPAM®. Add another one quarter of the potato salad, then cherry tomatoes. Finish with 2 more layers of potato salad separated by remaining SPAM®. Cover and refrigerate at least 2 hours to blend flavors. Before serving, garnish with green pepper rings and chopped radishes.

Pizza Heart

Makes 2 servings

   ⅔ cup diced cooked chicken
   1 tablespoon mayonnaise
   1 teaspoon minced onion
   ⅛ teaspoon prepared mustard
      Salt, pepper
      Pizza dough for 12-inch pizza
   ⅔ cup grated mozzarella cheese
   1 cup Ocean Spray Cranorange Cranberry
         Orange Sauce
   ⅓ cup sliced small green olives
   4 thin tomato slices, cut in half

Preheat oven to 425°F. In a bowl, combine chicken, mayonnaise, onion, and mustard. Season to taste with salt and pepper. Set aside. Place pizza dough on a greased 14-inch pizza pan. Using your fist, shape into a heart measuring 12 inches in height and width. Pinch point to obtain heart shape. Bake in oven for 10 to 12 minutes until thoroughly cooked but not brown. Remove crust from oven and cool. Sprinkle cheese around outer edge, leaving a rim of crust ½-inch wide. Spoon cranberry orange sauce inside cheese border. Place ol-ives in a single row inside cranberry orange sauce border. Shape into a heart and spread cranberry orange sauce to touch olives, if necessary. Arrange tomato half-slices inside olives, overlapping to fill entire center area. Spoon chicken salad onto tomato forming a heart shape. Bake until cheese is melted and pizza is hot, about 5 minutes.

Citrus Chicken Salad

Makes 7½ cups

   3 tablespoons all-purpose flour
   3 tablespoons sugar
   ½ teaspoon salt
   1 egg
   1 cup liquid Carnation Nonfat Dry Milk
   ½ cup orange juice
   4 cups cubed cooked chicken
   2 cups thinly sliced celery
   1 cup toasted slivered almonds
   1 cup fresh orange sections (about 3 medium
         oranges), or 1 cup (11-ounce can) mandarin
         orange sections
      Lettuce

Combine flour, sugar, and salt in medium saucepan. Blend in egg. Gradually stir in liquid nonfat milk and orange juice. Cook over medium heat, stirring constantly, until mixture just comes to a boil and thickens. Chill, stirring occasionally. Combine chicken, celery, almonds, orange sections, and dressing in medium bowl. Mix lightly but thoroughly. Chill. Serve on lettuce.

Baked Chicken Salad

Makes 4 to 6 servings

   1 cup potato chip crumbs (about 4 cups whole
         chips)
   2 cups diced cold chicken
   1½ cups sliced celery
   ½ cup Blender Mayonnaise (see index)
   1 cup cubed cheddar cheese
   1 slice lemon, seeded and peeled
   ½ small onion, cut in half
   ¼ cup almonds

Grease a 2-quart casserole. Crumb potato chips in blender. Reserve. Put chicken and celery into casserole. Put mayonnaise, cheddar cheese, lemon, and onion into blender; cover and process at Cream until smooth. Remove feeder cap; add almonds, processing only until chopped. Pour over chicken and celery, and mix. Sprinkle potato chip crumbs over top. Bake in a preheated 375°F. oven 30 minutes.

Hot Chicken Salad

Makes 4 servings

  2 cups diced cooked chicken
  1 can (8 ounces) water chestnuts, drained and sliced
  1 can (8 ounces) pineapple chunks, drained
  1 stalk celery, diced
  ½ cup mayonnaise
  1 tablespoon lemon juice
  ¾ teaspoon salt
  ¼ teaspoon ground ginger
  ½ cup toasted sliced almonds

Microwave: Combine chicken, water chestnuts, pineapple, and celery in 1½-quart casserole. Mix mayonnaise, lemon juice, salt, and ginger. Pour over chicken and toss to coat. Cover lightly with Saran Wrap, turning back edge to vent. Microcook at 90% power 8 minutes, stirring once. Sprinkle with toasted almonds and serve immediately.

Conventional: Preheat oven to 400°F. Combine chicken, water chestnuts, pineapple, and celery in 1½-quart casserole. Mix mayonnaise, lemon juice, salt, and ginger. Pour over chicken and toss to coat. Bake uncovered 20 minutes, or until top is lightly browned and casserole is bubbly. Serve as above.

Sunshine Chicken Salad

Makes 4 to 6 servings

  ¾ cup Libby's Solid Pack Pumpkin
  ½ cup mayonnaise
  1 teaspoon lemon juice
  1 teaspoon salt
  ¼ to ½ teaspoon dill weed
  ¼ teaspoon pepper
  ⅛ teaspoon garlic powder
  3 cups chopped cooked chicken
  1 cup chopped celery
  ½ cup chopped walnuts, toasted
  ¼ cup green onion slices

Combine pumpkin, mayonnaise, lemon juice, salt, dill weed, pepper, and garlic powder; mix well. Add remaining ingredients; mix lightly. Chill. Serve in tomato shells, avocado halves, pineapple boats, or split pita bread rounds, if desired.

Ruby Roll Chicken Salad

Makes 6 servings

  6 lasagna noodles
  1 cup Ocean Spray Cranberry Orange Sauce
  ¼ cup finely minced celery
  3 cups diced cooked chicken
  1 small red onion, thinly sliced
  1 can (11 ounces) mandarin oranges, drained
  1 package (10 ounces) frozen peas, thawed
    Black olives (optional)
  ¾ cup vegetable oil
  ¼ cup frozen concentrated orange juice, undiluted
  ½ teaspoon *each* paprika and dry mustard
  1 teaspoon salt
  ¼ teaspoon pepper
  1 clove garlic, mashed
    Shredded lettuce (about 6 cups)
    Black olives (optional)

In a large pan, cook lasagna noodles in boiling salted water until tender but still slightly firm. Drain and cover with cold water. In a small bowl, mix cranberry orange sauce with celery. Drain noodles and pat dry with paper towels. Spread noodles thinly with sauce mixture. Roll up each noodle like a jelly roll. Place seam side down on dish and cover with plastic wrap or foil. Chill. In a mixing bowl, combine chicken, onion, oranges, and peas. Set aside. In another mixing bowl, beat oil with orange juice, paprika, mustard, salt, pepper, and garlic until thick. Then pour over chicken mixture and toss to coat all pieces. Chill. When ready to serve, cover each serving plate with 1 cup shredded lettuce. Cut each lasagna roll crosswise into 3 thin slices. Place slices at outer edge of plates. Spoon chicken mixture in center of plate. Garnish, if desired, with black olives.

Mideastern Chicken Salad

Makes 4 servings

  1¼ cups chicken consommé
  1 cup walnuts
  4 blanched almonds
  1 teaspoon minced onion
  ¼ cup soft bread crumbs
  ½ teaspoon salt
  ½ teaspoon paprika
    Boston lettuce
  3 cups cubed cold cooked chicken
    Capers

Place first 7 ingredients in blender. Cover and process at Cream 1 minute. Place leaves of Boston lettuce on 4 serving plates and divide chicken over them. Spoon sauce over chicken. Sprinkle with capers.

Dilly of a Deli Salad (page 105). Photo courtesy of
Thomas J. Lipton, Inc.

Waldorf Chicken Salad with Honey Dressing

Makes 4 servings
- 2 cups cubed cooked chicken
- 2 medium-size red Delicious apples, cored and diced
- 1 cup seedless green or pitted Tokay grapes, cut in half
- ½ cup coarsely chopped walnuts, divided
- 3 tablespoons honey
- 4 tablespoons lemon juice
- ¼ cup vegetable oil
- ½ teaspoon tarragon
  Salt, freshly ground pepper to taste
- 2 small heads Bibb lettuce or 2 Belgian endives

Place chicken, apples, grapes, and ¼ cup chopped walnuts in medium-size bowl and toss gently. Place honey, lemon juice, oil, tarragon, salt, and pepper in screw-top jar and shake vigorously until thoroughly blended. Pour dressing over chicken mixture and mix gently until all ingredients are coated. Cover and refrigerate. Just before serving, line salad bowl with lettuce and spoon chicken mixture into center. Sprinkle remaining chopped walnuts over salad and serve immediately.

Ruby Roll Chicken Salad (page 109); Ham, Sweet Potato, and Orange Cranberry Salad (page 105); Greek Salad with Cheese Rolls (page 76).
Ocean Spray Cranberries

Hot Chef's Salad

Makes 4 to 6 servings
- ½ cup Italian dressing
- ½ tablespoon sugar
- 1 can (7 ounces) SPAM®, cut in strips
- 1 can (6¾ ounces) Hormel Chunk Chicken, drained and flaked
- 2 hard-cooked eggs, sliced
- ¼ cup sliced celery
- 2 cups lettuce, torn into bite-size pieces
- ¾ cup Swiss cheese, cut in julienne strips
- 1 small tomato, cut into thin wedges

In large skillet, combine dressing and sugar; heat to boiling. Layer SPAM®, chicken, eggs, celery, lettuce, cheese, and tomato in hot dressing; cover and cook over medium heat 5 minutes. Toss and serve immediately.

Chef's Salad Tout Chaud

Makes 6 to 8 servings
- ¾ cup Wish-Bone® Italian Dressing
- 1 tablespoon sugar
- 2 cups cooked ham, cut in julienne strips
- 2½ cups cut-up cooked chicken
- 4 hard-cooked eggs, sliced
- ½ cup sliced celery
- 3 cups lettuce, torn into bite-size pieces
- 1½ cups Swiss cheese, cut in julienne strips
- 1 large tomato, cut into thin wedges

In large skillet, combine Wish-Bone Italian Dressing and sugar; heat to boiling. Layer ham, chicken, eggs, celery, lettuce, cheese, and tomato in hot dressing; cover and cook over medium heat 5 minutes. Toss and serve immediately.

Tangy Chicken-Pineapple Salad

Makes 6 to 8 servings
- 1 small head iceberg lettuce, torn into pieces
- 2 cups shredded cooked chicken
- ¼ cup diced celery
- 1 can (13½ ounces) pineapple chunks, drained
  Salt, pepper to taste
- ¾ cup Wish-Bone® Chunky Blue Cheese Dressing

In salad bowl, combine lettuce, chicken, celery, pineapple, salt, and pepper; chill. Just before serving, toss with Wish-Bone Chunky Blue Cheese Dressing.

Main-Dish Salads

These go on picnics, of course. And they are just the thing for a summer luncheon or supper, or to take their place on a buffet table for a crowd. Here are some of the classics, both elegant and homey:

Sausage and kraut: Slice the sausage (kielbasa is good), combine with the kraut; season and dress with vinaigrette.

Beef: Julienne strips of rare roast beef, paper-thin onion rings, strips of dill pickle; olive oil and red wine vinegar combine for the dressing.

Jambon persilée (parslied ham): ⅔ ham chunks, ⅓ snipped parsley in a delicate, lemony white-wine gelatin.

Chicken: There are dozens of versions—with celery and minced onion, with fresh pineapple, with seedless grapes, with chopped walnuts, with capers and lemon mayonnaise, with roquefort-stuffed pitted fresh cherries are only a few.

Potato: Here, too, there are many—hot, with bacon dressing; cold made of half potatoes and half hard-cooked egg, or with lots of chopped dill pickle, or with onion and celery and slivers of ham, or with apples and curry dressing, and many, many more.

Niçoise: Bed of greens on a platter; arranged on it in separate heaps are vinaigrette-marinated cooked potatoes and green beans, tomatoes, tuna fish; decorated with anchovy fillets.

Chef's: Bed of mixed greens on which julienne strips of ham, chicken, and cheese, slices of hard-cooked egg, and wedges of tomato are laid in an attractive pattern.

Macaroni: Start out with cold, well-drained elbow macaroni or small seashells or any other chunky pasta you fancy; add all or some of these: chopped celery, chopped onion, sliced green olives, cheddar cheese cubes, ham slivers, pickle slices, chunks of hard-cooked egg, shredded red cabbage.

Shrimp: Plain or with celery and a bit of onion, dressed with green mayonnaise with plenty of lemon juice, or with lots of capers and plain lemon mayonnaise.

Salmon: Cold poached or canned salmon with celery, chives, cucumber, slices of sweet pickle.

Tomato Surprise: Making these for the first time, one home cook who was not a tomato lover was heard to say, "I'll be surprised if anyone eats them!"— but they're very good. Hollow out medium-size tomatoes and set upside down to drain; salt lightly, then fill with chicken, shrimp, or Russian salad.

Avocado Half-shells: Halve ripe avocados, fill the cavities with crab meat, shrimp, or chicken salad— chicken with a curry dressing is a particularly good choice.

Side-Dish Salad Ideas

Tossed green salad is not the only one. When you bog down, change the pace with one of these:

Waldorf: Apple chunks (don't peel them), diced celery, walnuts; another time, try pear chunks and pecans.

Sweet Carrot: ⅔ coarsely grated carrot, ⅓ raisins.

Slaw: Make it with green, napa, red, or Chinese cabbage; add pineapple chunks, seedless grapes, chopped peanuts, minced onion, grated carrot, slivered green peppers, or thin radish slices.

Russian—or call it French or Italian: Nobody's quite sure of the rightful claimant's name, but it's mixed cooked vegetables with plenty of minced garlic and chopped celery; dress it with mayonnaise or boiled dressing.

Spinach: Cartwheels of hard-cooked eggs and thin rings of red onion enliven the spinach; use hot bacon dressing.

Hearts of Lettuce: Sometimes the simple one is the best; top with roquefort or Russian dressing.

Stuffed Endive: Pale spears of Belgian endive stuffed with cream cheese and chives, served on lettuce leaves.

White Bean: ½ drained (canned) white beans, ½ a combination of chopped celery, sliced scallions; season well, toss with olive oil and white wine vinegar.

Beets and Red Dutch Eggs: Beet and onion slices in a dressing of oil and vinegar and a dash of cloves, with part of the beet liquid; immerse peeled hard-cooked eggs in the liquid; let stand 24 hours.

Pawnbrokers' Special: Balls of three kinds of melon—honeydew, watermelon, and cantaloupe— with honey-lime dressing or half-and-half sour cream and mayonnaise.

Fodder: Alfalfa sprouts, pine nuts, and shredded lettuce.

Caesar: Romaine, croutons, cut-up anchovy fillets, with its own special dressing of a raw or coddled egg, garlic-flavored olive oil, lemon juice, salt, pepper, and mustard, the whole deal sprinkled with Parmesan.

Asparagus Vinaigrette: That's it—cold cooked asparagus marinated for several hours in French dressing.

Scallion or Leek: Same thing with cooked scallions or leeks.

Artichoke: Cold cooked artichoke with French dressing into which to dip the leaves; or cook, cool, and marinate artichoke hearts.

Green Bean: Cold cooked green beans, Lorenzo dressing.

Apple-Turkey Toss

Makes 6 servings

    2 cups cubed cooked Armour Golden Star
        Boneless Young Turkey
    2 cups chopped apples
    1 cup sliced celery
    ⅔ cup mayonnaise
    ¼ cup slivered almonds
    2 tablespoons lemon juice
    ½ teaspoon basil leaves, crushed
    ½ teaspoon ground sage
    ½ teaspoon salt
        Lettuce cups
    2 hard-cooked eggs, sliced

Combine all ingredients except eggs and lettuce; toss lightly. Spoon into lettuce cups. Top with eggs.

Gala Turkey Salad Toss

Makes 6 servings

    1 medium head iceberg lettuce, torn into pieces
    1 tomato, cut in wedges
    1 green pepper, diced
    3 green onions, sliced
    1 cup cut-up cooked turkey or chicken
    ½ cup sliced celery
    1 cup seasoned croutons
    ½ cup Wish-Bone® Chunky Blue Cheese Dressing

In salad bowl, arrange lettuce, tomato, green pepper, green onions, turkey, and celery; chill. Just before serving, toss with croutons and Wish-Bone Chunky Blue Cheese Dressing.

Turkey-Fruit Toss

Makes 4 servings

    2 cups cubed cooked Armour Golden Star
        Boneless Young Turkey
    3 bananas, sliced
    ½ cup chopped celery
    ½ cup chopped pecans
    ½ cup mayonnaise
    2 tablespoons finely chopped onion
    2 teaspoons lemon juice
    1 teaspoon salt
    ¼ teaspoon dill weed
        Dash pepper
        Lettuce cups
        Jellied cranberry sauce

In large bowl, combine all ingredients except lettuce and cranberry sauce. Cover; chill until ready to serve. Spoon mixture into lettuce cups; top each serving with cranberry sauce.

Peanut Super Supper Salad

Makes 8 cups salad

    ½ cup vegetable oil
    3 tablespoons fresh lemon juice
    2 tablespoons white vinegar
    1 teaspoon sugar
    1 teaspoon coriander seed, crushed
    1 teaspoon cumin seed, crushed
    1 clove garlic, crushed
    ½ teaspoon salt
        Dash cayenne
    8 cups torn-up lettuce and fresh spinach
    2 cups sliced fresh mushrooms (about ½ pound)
    2 cups leftover cooked pork, chicken, ham, or
        beef, cut in julienne strips
    1½ cups cocktail peanuts
        Lettuce cups
        Onion rings

In a small glass jar, shake together oil, lemon juice, vinegar, sugar, coriander, cumin, garlic, salt, and cayenne. Chill. Just before serving, toss together salad greens, mushrooms, meat, and peanuts. Pour dressing over salad and toss to coat. Serve salad in a lettuce cup garnished with onion rings.

Thousand Island Chicken Salad

Makes about 4 servings

    ½ cup Wish-Bone® Thousand Island Dressing
    2 cups shredded cooked chicken
    ½ cup diced celery
    ¼ cup coarsely chopped walnuts
        Salt and pepper to taste
        Lettuce leaves (optional)

In large bowl, combine all ingredients; chill. Serve, if desired, on lettuce or as a sandwich spread.

Chick 'n' Bacon Salad

Makes about 4 servings

    2 cups cut-up cooked chicken
    6 slices bacon, crisp-cooked and crumbled
    2 medium carrots, thinly sliced
    2 medium tomatoes, cut into wedges
    ½ cup sliced celery
    1 medium head romaine lettuce, torn into pieces
    ½ cup Wish-Bone® Italian or Robusto Italian
        Dressing

In large bowl, arrange chicken, bacon, carrots, tomatoes, and celery on lettuce; chill. Just before serving, toss with Wish-Bone Italian Dressing.

Chinese-Style Chicken Salad.

Molded Chicken Salad

Makes 6 servings

     2 tablespoons dry sherry
     1 teaspoon lemon juice
     1 envelope unflavored gelatin
     ½ cup boiling chicken broth, or ½ chicken bouil-
          lon cube dissolved in ½ cup boiling water
     ¼ cup mayonnaise
     ¼ teaspoon dry mustard
          Few dashes hot pepper sauce
     2 sprigs parsley
     1 thin slice onion
     ½ green pepper, seeded and cut up
     3 stalks celery, cut up
     1 canned pimiento, cut up
     2 cups cubed cooked chicken
          Salad greens

   Put sherry and lemon juice into blender container.
Sprinkle on gelatin; let stand 1 minute. Add boiling
broth. Cover; blend at low speed until gelatin is dissolved. Add remaining ingredients except chicken and
salad greens in order listed. Cover; blend at medium
speed just until vegetables are coarsely chopped. Add
chicken. Cover; blend at medium speed just until all
chicken goes through blades. If necessary, stop blender
during processing and push ingredients toward blades
with rubber spatula. Pour into 1½-quart mold or
9x5x3-inch loaf pan. Chill several hours or until firm.
Unmold onto salad greens.

Chinese-Style Chicken Salad

Makes 6 servings

     2 chicken breasts, skinned and boned
          Soy sauce
     4 tablespoons cooking oil, divided
     1 clove garlic, minced
     1 teaspoon grated, lemon rind, divided
     1 tablespoon lemon juice
     ½ teaspoon salt
     4 cups torn spinach leaves
     4 cups thinly sliced Chinese cabbage
     2 tablespoons sesame seed, toasted

   Cut chicken into ½-inch strips. Combine 1 tablespoon soy sauce, 2 tablespoons oil, garlic, and ½ teaspoon lemon rind. Spoon mixture over chicken.
Marinate in refrigerator at least 2 hours, turning occasionally. Drain chicken. In skillet, heat 1 tablespoon oil
and sauté chicken until lightly browned. Refrigerate.
When ready to serve, combine remaining oil, 1 teaspoon soy sauce, remaining lemon rind, lemon juice,
and salt. Combine spinach and Chinese cabbage; pour
dressing over vegetable mixture and toss. Add chicken
and sesame seed and toss again.

Festive Salad (page 108). Courtesy of Geo. A. Hormel & Co.

Family Curried Salad Plate

Makes 4 servings

   2 nectarines, peaches, or plums, peeled and sliced
   2 cups cantaloupe, honeydew, or watermelon
        balls
   1 avocado, pared and sliced
   1 medium cucumber, cut in spears, or 2 cups
        salad greens, torn into bite-size pieces
   1 tomato, cut in wedges, or 1 cup cherry
        tomatoes
  12 whole radishes or seedless green grapes
   1 small red onion, thinly sliced, or 8 scallions,
        trimmed
   1 green pepper, seeded and cut in strips
  ½ pound cooked chicken, turkey, ham, or other
        luncheon meat, thinly sliced
  ½ pound sliced Swiss, American, or Muenster
        cheese
        Creamy Curry Dressing (recipe follows)
        Whole grain bread

On a large platter, arrange fruits, vegetables, and sliced meat and cheese. Serve with Creamy Curry Dressing and slices of whole grain bread.

Creamy Curry Dressing

Makes 1 cup

  ½ cup sour cream
  ½ cup mayonnaise
   1 tablespoon honey
  ¼ to ½ teaspoon curry powder
  ⅛ teaspoon salt

In a small bowl, stir all ingredients until smooth.

Q. *I'm not much of a one for gadgets, such as separate choppers for nuts, onions, etc. But there must be a better way to chop an onion than to cut it into slices and then cut each slice into pieces. Is there? How about other vegetables?*

A. There is. Peel an onion and cut it in half lengthwise. Place it on a chopping board cutside down, with the root end to your left, holding it in place with your left hand. With a sharp knife, cut several slices parallel to the board from tip to, but not through, the root end. Now make several cuts, to but not through the root end, at right angles to the cutting board and to the previous cuts. Now slice the half onion at the root, and neat pieces will fall in front of your knife. For minced onions, make all cuts as close together as possible. For chopped or diced, make the cuts proportionately farther apart.

Cut celery, seeded cucumber, green pepper, and carrots into long thin strips. Hold a bundle of strips with your left hand. Cut across the strips into small pieces, regulating the size by whether the recipe calls for the vegetable to be minced, diced, or chopped.

Bonus: To acquire a small amount—a tablespoon or two—of parsley watercress, or chives, hold a bundle of sprigs in your left hand, snip off bits of the vegetables with kitchen scissors.

Italian Tuna Toss Salad (page 121). Ralston Purina Company

Tomato Flowers with Seafood Salad

Makes 6 servings

  1 can (7 ounces) crab meat or tuna, drained
  1 cup sliced celery
  ¼ pound mushrooms, sliced
  ½ cup Wish-Bone® Creamy Italian Dressing
  2 tablespoons chili sauce
  6 small tomatoes

In medium bowl, combine crab, celery, and mushrooms; toss with Wish-Bone Creamy Italian Dressing blended with chili sauce and chill. Meanwhile, cut tomatoes almost completely through into wedges; spread apart to form flowers. Just before serving, spoon salad mixture onto centers of tomatoes.

Capers

The unopened flower buds of a shrub native to the Mediterranean, capers are preserved in vinegar with a touch of salt. They add piquant flavor to salads of several kinds. One superb salad combines cold poached chicken breast masked with homemade lemon mayonnaise and sprinkled with capers—simple, but perfect.

Use capers as a garnish for salads, or as an enlivener in salad fillings for sandwiches.

Buy capers in small glass jars, refrigerate after opening. They can be stored for at least 6 months. The smaller the bud, the better the flavor—and the more expensive.

Tasty Tuna Salad in Pepper Cups

Makes 4 servings

  4 large green peppers
  1 can (7 ounces) tuna, drained and flaked
1¼ cups chopped celery
  ½ cup sliced radishes
  ¼ cup sweet pickle relish
  ⅓ cup Wish-Bone® Italian Dressing

Cut thin slice off top of peppers and remove stems and seeds, to form cups. In medium bowl, combine tuna, celery, radishes, and relish; add Wish-Bone Italian Dressing and toss thoroughly. Spoon mixture into pepper cups; wrap and chill.

Fruited Tuna Salad with Cucumber Dressing

Makes 2 servings

  1 can (6½ ounces) Bumble Bee Chunk Light
      Tuna in Water
  1 quart shredded lettuce
  1 firm large Dole banana, peeled and sliced
  1 green pepper, seeded and chopped
  1 can (11 ounces) mandarin oranges
  ½ cup thinly sliced radishes
  1 tablespoon toasted sesame seed
      Cucumber Dressing (recipe follows)

Drain tuna. Arrange lettuce on a round platter. Place tuna in center. Arrange banana, pepper, oranges, and radishes around tuna. Sprinkle with sesame seed. Serve with Cucumber Dressing.

Cucumber Dressing

  ¼ cup peeled minced cucumber
  ¼ cup cider vinegar
  2 tablespoons vegetable oil
  2 tablespoons sugar
  ½ teaspoon prepared hot mustard

Combine all ingredients in a screw-top jar. Shake well. Serve over salad.

Elegant Tuna and Pears

Makes 2 servings

  1 can (6½ ounces) Bumble Bee Chunk Light
      Tuna in Water
  ½ cup chopped ripe pear
  ⅓ cup sliced green onion
  ¼ cup sour cream
  ½ teaspoon *fines herbes,* crumbled
  ¼ teaspoon celery salt
  1 large cantaloupe
      Crisp salad greens
      Parsley sprigs
      Assorted fruits in season

Drain tuna. Combine with pear, green onion, sour cream, *fines herbes,* and celery salt. Slice cantaloupe in half; remove seeds. Mound tuna mixture in centers of each half. Place cantaloupe on salad plates lined with crisp salad greens. Garnish with parsley and serve with favorite fruits in season.

Salade Niçoise

Makes 4 servings

2 tablespoons white vinegar
2 tablespoons Dijon mustard
⅓ cup Mazola Corn Oil
⅓ cup skim milk
1 tablespoon chopped parsley
½ teaspoon sugar
¼ teaspoon salt
Dash pepper
4 cups torn lettuce leaves (½ pound)
1 can (7 ounces) tuna packed in water, drained and flaked
2 cups whole green beans, cook tender-crisp, chilled
4 new potatoes, cooked, sliced (about ½ pound)
1 tomato, cut in wedges
1 small red onion, thinly sliced, separated into rings

Place vinegar and mustard in blender container; cover. Blend on medium speed 20 seconds, or until well mixed. With blender running, slowly pour in corn oil. If necessary, stop blender during processing and push ingredients toward blades with rubber spatula. With blender running slowly, pour in milk. Add parsley, sugar, salt, and pepper; cover. Blend on medium speed 20 seconds, or until well mixed. Cover; refrigerate. Place lettuce on large serving platter. Arrange tuna, green beans, potatoes, tomato, and onion on lettuce. Serve with dressing.

Note: Use 2 tablespoon dressing per serving. Remaining dressing may be stored in tightly covered container in refrigerator up to 1 week. Dressing can also be served with cold meats, fish, or other vegetables.

Salade Niçoise à la Wish-Bone

Makes about 4 servings

2 quarts mixed salad greens
4 cups sliced cooked potatoes (about 6 medium)
3 cups cooked cut-up green beans (about ¾ pound)
1 can (9¼ ounces) chunk tuna, drained
4 hard-cooked eggs, quartered
2 medium tomatoes, cut into wedges
½ cup pitted ripe olives
1 can (2 ounces) anchovy fillets
1 cup (8 ounces) Wish-Bone® Sweet 'n Spicy French or Deluxe French Dressing

On serving platter arrange salad greens, potatoes, green beans, tuna, eggs, tomatoes, olives, and anchovies; chill. Just before serving, pour Wish-Bone Sweet 'n Spicy French Dressing over salad.

Treasure Valley Tuna-Potato Salad

Makes 4 to 6 servings

1 package (5.5 ounces) Idaho® Hash Brown Potatoes
1¾ cups boiling water
Dressing (recipe follows)
2 tomatoes, cut into eighths
1 can (1 pound) cut green beans, drained
1 head romaine lettuce
1 can (6 ounces) pitted ripe olives, drained
4 hard-cooked eggs, cut in quarters
2 cans (6½ or 7 ounces each) tuna, drained

Place hash brown potatoes in mixing bowl. Add boiling water; let stand until water is absorbed, about 10 minutes. Pour ½ cup dressing over potatoes; cover and refrigerate several hours. Put tomatoes and green beans in separate bowls; add ¼ cup dressing to each bowl. Cover and refrigerate several hours. At serving time, line platter with lettuce leaves. Arrange potatoes, tomatoes, green beans, olives, eggs, and tuna on lettuce leaves. Serve with remaining dressing.

Dressing

1⅓ cups salad oil
¼ cup lemon juice
¼ cup tarragon vinegar
2 teaspoons salt
2 teaspoons grated onion
1 teaspoon dry mustard
1 teaspoon dried basil
¼ teaspoon pepper

In a small bowl, beat all ingredients until well mixed.

Tuna Deluxe Salad

Makes about 6 servings

1 small head iceberg lettuce, torn into pieces
½ head romaine lettuce, torn into pieces
2 cans (7 ounces each) tuna, drained and flaked
½ pound fresh mushrooms, sliced
2 tomatoes, cut into wedges
1 green pepper, cut into rings
¾ cup Wish-Bone® Italian or Deluxe French Dressing

In salad bowl, arrange lettuces, tuna, mushrooms, tomatoes, and green pepper; chill. Just before serving, toss with Wish-Bone Italian Dressing.

Crab Meat-Avocado Salad

Makes 2 servings

- 1 **avocado**
- ½ **lemon**
- ½ **cup mayonnaise**
- ¼ **cup ketchup**
- 2 **tablespoons finely chopped pickle**
- 1 **tablespoon snipped parsley**
- 1 **tablespoon chopped dill**
  Salt and pepper to taste
- 8 **ounces crab meat, flaked**

Cut avocado in half and discard pit; rub with lemon to prevent discoloration. Mix mayonnaise, ketchup, pickle, parsley, dill, salt, and pepper until blended; squeeze in rest of juice from lemon. Heap crab meat chunks in avocado; top with mayonnaise-ketchup.

Crab Meat-Avocado Salad

Tossed Green Salad with Clam Dressing

Makes about 6 servings salad and 1½ cups dressing
- ½ cup lemon juice
- ¼ cup Doxsee Clam Juice
- ¼ cup tomato juice
- 4 ounces Doxsee Minced Clams
  Artificial sweetener equal to ¼ cup sugar
- 1 teaspoon dry mustard
- ½ teaspoon salt
- ⅛ teaspoon pepper
- 6 cups mixed salad greens, torn into bite-size pieces
- ½ pound bacon, cooked and crumbled

Combine all ingredients except salad greens and bacon. Blend well. Chill dressing. When ready to serve salad, toss greens with dressing, then toss quickly with bacon.

Scandinavian Salmon Salad

Makes about 4 servings
- ¾ cup Wish-Bone® Creamy Cucumber Dressing
- 1 can (7¾ ounces) salmon, drained and flaked
- ¼ cup sliced celery
  Lettuce (optional)
  Lemon wedges (optional)

In medium bowl, combine Wish-Bone Creamy Cucumber Dressing with salmon, celery, and onion; chill. Serve, if desired, on lettuce with lemon wedges.

New England Clam Chowder (page 39); Tossed Green Salad with Clam Dressing. © Doxsee Food Corp.

Savory Shrimp Salad

Makes 4 servings
 1 **cup Hellmann's or Best Foods Real Mayonnaise**
 ½ **cup chopped green onions**
 ½ **cup chopped parsley**
 2 **tablespoons lemon juice**
 1 **teaspoon sugar**
 ¼ **teaspoon salt**
 1 **pound shrimp, cooked, cleaned, and chilled**
    Avocado and tomato wedges
    Lemon slices

In small bowl, stir together first 6 ingredients. Cover; chill at least 2 hours. Serve shrimp and dressing on avocado and tomato wedges. Garnish with lemon slices.

Jambalaya Salad

Makes about 6 servings
 1 **cup (8 ounces) Wish-Bone® Sweet 'n Spicy**
    French Dressing
 1 **cup sour cream**
 1 **tablespoon chili powder**
 4 **cups chilled cooked rice**
 1½ **pounds (about 5 cups) cut-up cooked chicken,**
    ham, or shrimp
 2 **medium tomatoes, cut into wedges**
 1 **medium green pepper, cut into chunks**
 1 **cup sliced celery**

In medium bowl, blend Wish-Bone Sweet 'n Spicy French Dressing, sour cream, and chili powder; chill. On large platter, arrange rice, chicken, tomatoes, green pepper, and celery; serve with dressing.

Tropical Sea Salad

Makes 4 to 6 servings
 1 **head red romaine, sliced into bite-size pieces**
 ½ **pound cooked crab meat, shredded**
 1 **Red Delicious apple, cored and chopped with**
    peel
 1 **soft Calavo mango, peeled, seeded, and diced**
 1 **tablespoon capers, drained**
 ¼ **cup prepared Italian dressing**

Place romaine in large salad bowl; add crab meat, apple, mango, and capers. Pour dressing over salad bowl ingredients; toss well to blend. Serve immediately.

Shrimp-Cucumber Salad

Makes 4 to 6 servings
 1 **pound shrimp, cleaned and cooked**
 ½ **cup thinly sliced celery**
 ¼ **medium green pepper, thinly sliced**
 ¾ **cup Wish-Bone® Creamy Cucumber Dressing**
 2 **teaspoons lemon juice**
    Lettuce cups

In medium bowl, combine shrimp, celery, and green pepper; chill. Just before serving, blend creamy cucumber dressing and lemon juice; toss with shrimp mixture. Serve on lettuce cups.

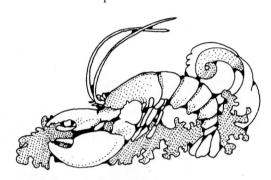

Fresh-as-Spring Shrimp Mold

Makes about 6 servings
 2 **envelopes Knox® Unflavored Gelatine**
 2 **tablespoons sugar**
 1½ **cups boiling water**
 1 **cup mayonnaise**
 ¼ **cup Wish-Bone® Italian Dressing**
 3 **tablespoons lemon juice**
 1½ **cups chopped cooked asparagus**
 1 **cup chopped cooked shrimp**
 ½ **cup chopped tomato**
 1½ **tablespoons finely chopped onion**
    Tomato wedges (optional)

In a medium bowl, mix Knox Unflavored Gelatine with sugar. Add boiling water and stir until gelatine is completely dissolved. With wire whip or rotary beater, blend in mayonnaise, Wish-Bone Italian Dressing, and lemon juice. Chill, stirring occasionally, until mixture is the consistency of unbeaten egg whites. Fold in remaining ingredients except tomato wedges. Turn mixture into a 9-inch layer cake pan and chill until firm, about 4 hours. Unmold to serve. Garnish with tomato wedges, if desired.

Italian Tuna Toss Salad

Makes 6 servings

- ¼ cup olive oil
- 2 tablespoons white wine vinegar
- 1 clove garlic, minced
- ½ teaspoon basil leaves, crushed
- ⅛ teaspoon dry mustard
  - Dash ground black pepper
- 1½ cups torn salad greens
- ½ small cucumber, thinly sliced
- ½ cup bite-size cauliflowerets
- 4 radishes, sliced
- 2 green onions, thinly sliced
- 3 tablespoons shredded carrot
- 1 can (6½ ounces) Chicken of the Sea® Chunk Light Tuna with 50% less salt, drained★
- 1 medium-size tomato, cut into eights

In small bowl, combine oil, vinegar, garlic, basil, dry mustard, and pepper. Cover. Refrigerate 1 to 2 hours. In large salad, bowl, toss salad greens, cucumber, cauliflower, radishes, onion, and carrot. Just before serving, pour oil-and-vinegar mixture over vegetables. Toss. Add tuna and tomato. Toss lightly.

★Tuna packed in oil or water may be used, based on personal preference.

Crab Mousse in Tomato Cups

Makes 8 to 12 servings

- 1 envelope unflavored gelatine
- ½ cup cold water
- 2 tablespoons sugar
- 2 teaspoons salt
- 2 teaspoons dry mustard
- ½ cup fresh lemon juice
- ½ cup sour cream
- 2 cups flaked cooked crab
- ¼ cup snipped fresh dill
- ½ cup heavy cream, whipped
- 8 to 12 large tomatoes
  - Dill sprigs

Sprinkle gelatin over water in saucepan. Place over low heat; stir constantly until gelatin dissolves, about 3 minutes. Remove from heat. Stir in sugar, salt, dry mustard, and lemon juice. Add sour cream and beat until blended. Chill, stirring occasionally, until mixture mounds slightly when dropped from a spoon. Stir in flaked crab and dill. Fold in whipped cream. Chill until mixture can be piled in mounds. Remove thin slice from top of tomato and scoop out pulp to form a shell. Reserve tomato pulp for soup, sauce, or stuffing other vegetables. Drain liquid from tomato shells. Spoon in chilled crab mousse, piling high over top of tomato. Chill until firm, 3 or 4 hours. Garnish with sprigs of dill.

Molded Clam and Tomato Ring

Makes 6 servings

- 2 envelopes unflavored gelatin
- ½ cup cold water
- 1 can (10½ ounces) minced clams
- 1½ teaspoons Lea & Perrins Worcestershire Sauce
- 2¾ cups tomato juice
- 1 cup thinly sliced celery
- ¼ cup sliced scallions

Soften gelatin in water for 5 minutes. Drain clams, reserving liquid and clams separately. Add sufficient water to clam liquid to make ¾ cup. In a small saucepan, heat clam liquid and Lea & Perrins just to the boiling point. Pour over gelatin; stir to dissolve. Add tomato juice. Chill until mixture thickens to consistency of unbeaten egg white. Stir in reserved clams, celery, and scallions. Pour into a 5-cup ring mold. Chill until firm. Unmold onto serving platter.

Festive Guacamole Grapefruit Salad

Makes 10 to 12 servings

- 2 envelopes unflavored gelatin
- ½ cup cold water
- 1½ cups boiling water
- 2¼ teaspoons salt
- 2 teaspoons fresh grated grapefruit peel
- 2 teaspoons grated onion
- 2 tablespoons fresh-squeezed lemon juice
- ¼ cup fresh-squeezed grapefruit juice
- 4 large soft-ripe avocados (3 cups mashed)
- ¾ cup mayonnaise (not salad dressing)
- 3 to 4 tablespoons finely chopped green chilies, or 5 to 6 drops hot pepper sauce
- 3 to 4 large Sunkist® grapefruit, sectioned and seeded
- 1 pound medium shrimp, cooked, shelled, and deveined

Soften gelatin in cold water for 5 minutes; stir in boiling water until thoroughly dissolved. Cool slightly; add salt, peel, onion, lemon, and grapefruit juice. Chill until completely cool but still liquid. Meanwhile, cut avocado into chunks; beat with electric or rotary beater in deep bowl until smooth and creamy. Beat in mayonnaise. Stir in chilies; then gradually stir in cool gelatin mixture until blended. Pour into 6-cup ring mold; chill until firm. When ready to serve, unmold on serving plate; fill center with chilled grapefruit sections and chilled cooked shrimp.

Variation

If shrimp is too much for your budget, try substituting white tuna, pink salmon, or diced cooked chicken.

What the Well-Dressed Salad Wears

You went to the trouble to toss up a super salad—now add the crowning touch, your own incomparable homemade dressing.

Thousand Island Dressing

Makes about 1½ cups

  1 **cup Hellmann's or Best Foods Real Mayonnaise**
  ⅓ **cup chili sauce or catsup**
  ⅓ **cup finely chopped celery (optional)**
  3 **tablespoons sweet pickle relish**
  1 **hard-cooked egg, chopped**

In small bowl, stir together mayonnaise, chili sauce, celery, pickle relish, and egg until well blended. Cover; refrigerate at least 2 hours to blend flavors.

Creamy Blue Cheese Dressing

Makes about 1½ cups

  1 **cup Hellmann's or Best Foods Real Mayonnaise**
  4 **ounces blue cheese, crumbled**
  3 **tablespoons milk**
  2 **tablespoons lemon juice or dry white wine**
  1 **tablespoon finely chopped onion**
  2 **teaspoons sugar**
  ¼ **teaspoon salt**
  ¼ **teaspoon dry mustard**
  ¼ **teaspoon Worcestershire sauce**

In small bowl, stir together mayonnaise, cheese, milk, lemon juice, onion, sugar, salt, mustard, and Worcestershire sauce until well blended. Cover; refrigerate at least 2 hours to blend flavors.

Russian Dressing

Makes about 1½ cups

  1 **cup Hellmann's or Best Foods Real Mayonnaise**
  ⅓ **cup chili sauce or catsup**
  ⅓ **cup chopped pickles**
  2 **teaspoons lemon juice**
  2 **teaspoons sugar**

In small bowl, stir together mayonnaise, chili sauce, pickles. lemon juice, and sugar until well blended. Cover; refrigerate at least 2 hours to blend flavors.

Creamy French Dressing

Makes about 1¼ cups

  1 **cup Hellmann's or Best Foods Real Mayonnaise**
  2 **tablespoons lemon juice or vinegar**
  4 **teaspoons sugar**
  1 **tablespoon milk**
  1 **teaspoon paprika**
  ½ **teaspoon dry mustard**
  ¼ **teaspoon salt**
  ⅛ **teaspoon pepper**

In small bowl, stir together mayonnaise, lemon juice, sugar, milk, paprika, mustard, salt, and pepper until well blended. Cover; refrigerate at least 2 hours to blend flavors.

Creamy Italian Dressing

Makes about 1 cup

  1 **cup Hellmann's or Best Foods Real Mayonnaise**
  2 **tablespoons grated Parmesan cheese**
  2 **tablespoons red wine vinegar**
  1 **small clove garlic, minced or pressed**
  ⅛ **teaspoon dried oregano leaves**

In small bowl, stir together mayonnaise, cheese, vinegar, garlic, and oregano until well blended. Cover; refrigerate at least 2 hours to blend flavors.

Creamy Italian Dressing; Creamy French Dressing; Creamy Blue Cheese Dressing; Russian Dressing; Thousand Island Dressing.
Hellmann's/Best Foods Real Mayonnaise

Mayonnaise

Makes 2 cups
  1 egg
  1 egg yolk
  ¾ teaspoon salt
  ¾ teaspoon dry mustard
  2 tablespoons lemon juice
  1 tablespoon vinegar
  1½ cups vegetable oil

Put egg, egg yolk, salt, mustard, lemon juice, vinegar, and ½ cup oil into blender container. Cover; blend at high speed until mixed. While blender is running, tip center cap and add remaining 1 cup oil in a slow, steady stream.

Mayonnaise Chaud-Froid

Sprinkle 1 envelope unflavored gelatin over ¼ cup cold water in small bowl. Let stand 5 minutes. Set bowl over boiling water; stir until gelatin is dissolved. Put gelatin mixture and 1 cup mayonnaise into blender container. Cover; blend at high speed until smooth. Use to coat eggs, ham, chicken, fish, etc.

Note: If mayonnaise separates or is too thin, the ingredients may not have been at room temperature or the oil may have been added too rapidly, causing the emulsion to break. However, you can easily salvage the ingredients. Pour the broken emulsion into a pitcher or other container. Wash and dry blender container. Break 1 egg into container; cover and run on low speed. While blender is running, slowly add the broken emulsion. When mixture reaches top of blender blades, run on high speed, continuing to add the separated mayonnaise slowly.

Blender Mayonnaise

Makes 1½ cups
  1 egg
  2 tablespoons lemon juice
  1 piece lemon rind
  ½ teaspoon dry mustard
  1 teaspoon salt
  1 cup salad oil

Place egg and lemon juice in blender. Using a vegetable peeler, cut off a strip of lemon rind. Add to blender along with mustard, salt, and ¼ cup oil. Cover, process at Crush 6 seconds. Remove feeder cap; add remaining oil in a thin stream. Turn off blender; serve at once or refrigerate.

Variations

For Tarragon Mayonnaise, omit lemon juice and rind, substitute 2 tablespoons tarragon vinegar. For Tomato Mayonnaise, add 2 tablespoons tomato paste with egg and lemon juice, an extra ¼ teaspoon salt, and ¼ teaspoon white pepper. For Curry Mayonnaise, substitute 2 tablespoons cider vinegar for lemon juice and rind; add 1 teaspoon curry powder before processing.

Vinaigrette Dressing

Makes about ¾ cup
  ½ cup oil
  3 tablespoons vinegar
  1½ teaspoons Lea & Perrins Worcestershire Sauce
  1½ teaspoons parsley flakes
  ¼ teaspoon garlic powder
  Salt and pepper to taste

Combine all ingredients. Toss with greens.

Caesar Dressing

Makes 1¼ cups
  1 cup Hellmann's or Best Foods Real Mayonnaise
  3 tablespoons milk
  2 tablespoons cider vinegar
  2 tablespoons grated Parmesan cheese
  ½ teaspoon sugar
  ⅛ teaspoon garlic powder

Stir ingredients together. Cover; chill.

Green Goddess Salad Dressing

Makes 2 cups
  1 cup mayonnaise
  ½ cup sour cream
  1 can (2 ounces) anchovy fillets, drained
  ¼ cup chopped parsley
  1 tablespoon minced onion
  ½ teaspoon tarragon leaves, crumbled
  ⅛ teaspoon salt
  2 tablespoons wine vinegar
  1 tablespoon lemon juice
  1 tablespoon Lea & Perrins Worcestershire Sauce
  1 small clove garlic

In the container of an electric blender combine all ingredients. Blend until smooth, about 1 to 2 minutes.

Low-Cal Yogurt Salad Dressing

Makes 1¼ cups
  2 tablespoons lemon juice
  2 tablespoons catsup
  2 teaspoons Lea & Perrins Worcestershire Sauce
  ¼ teaspoon garlic powder
  1 cup (8 ounces) plain yogurt
  Salt (optional)

In a small mixing bowl, combine lemon juice, catsup, Lea & Perrins, and garlic powder; blend. Stir in yogurt. Add salt to taste, if desired. Serve over torn salad greens or mixed vegetables.

Horseradish Cream Dressing

Makes about 1 cup

   ¼ cup heavy cream, whipped
   1 tablespoon lemon juice
   1 or 2 tablespoons prepared Gold's Horseradish
   ⅛ teaspoon salt
   ⅛ teaspoon paprika

Into the whipped cream fold remaining ingredients; toss with salad.

Sweet-Sour Salad Dressing

Makes about 2 cups

   4 slices bacon
   2 tablespoons finely chopped onion
   ¼ cup Sue Bee Honey
   ¼ cup vinegar
   ½ cup water
   1 cup bottled Italian-style salad dressing

Fry bacon until crisp. Remove bacon, drain on paper towel, and crumble into small pieces. Set aside. Sauté onion in bacon drippings until tender. Pour off all but 1 tablespoon of the drippings. Add honey, vinegar, and water. Bring to a boil. Cool. Combine mixture with salad dressing and beat or blend. Stir in bacon pieces. Chill. Shake well before using.

Lorenzo Dressing

Makes 1¾ cups

   1 cup Star Olive Oil
   ¼ cup Star Red Wine Vinegar
   1 teaspoon salt
   ½ teaspoon freshly ground pepper
   ¼ cup chili sauce
   ¼ cup chopped watercress
   ¼ teaspoon paprika

Mix all ingredients together and chill.

Creamy Garlic Dressing

Makes 2 cups

   ¼ cup lemon juice
   ¾ cup salad oil
   ⅔ cup light cream
   2 cloves garlic
   1 teaspoon salt
   ½ teaspoon sugar
   ¼ teaspoon white pepper
   ½ teaspoon paprika

Put all ingredients into blender; cover and process at Whip until blended.

Red Roquefort Dressing

Makes about 1 cup

   3 ounces Roquefort cheese
   ¼ cup catsup
   ¼ cup mayonnaise
   1 tablespoon chopped parsley
   1 tablespoon heavy cream

With wooden spoon, blend ingredients together well. Chill for about 15 minutes and serve on fruit or vegetable salad or with cold meats.

Buttermilk Blue Cheese Dressing

Makes 4 cups

   1 cup buttermilk
   2 cups mayonnaise
   ½ small onion, cut up
   1 tablespoon Worcestershire sauce
   ¼ teaspoon garlic powder
   ½ pound blue cheese, crumbled

Put buttermilk, mayonnaise, onion, Worcestershire sauce, garlic powder, and half the cheese into blender container. Cover; blend at high speed until smooth. Add remaining cheese. Cover; blend at low speed until mixed. If a smooth dressing is preferred, blend until smooth.

Old-Fashioned Cooked Salad Dressing

Makes 2½ cups

   1 teaspoon salt
   3 teaspoons dry mustard
   1 teaspoon powdered onion
   4 teaspoons all-purpose flour
   4 tablespoons sugar
   2 large eggs
   ⅔ cup cider vinegar
   1 cup light cream
   1 tablespoon butter or margarine, softened
     Salt and pepper

Combine first 5 ingredients in small Sunbeam Mixmaster Mixer bowl. Add eggs. Beat at medium until completely blended. Turn Mixer to lowest speed; beat in vinegar, then cream. Transfer to heavy saucepan and cook over low heat, stirring constantly, until thickened. Remove from heat and stir in butter. Season to taste with salt and pepper. Refrigerate.

Jade Dressing. Courtesy of Colombo, Inc.

Jade Dressing

Makes 18 tablespoons
   1 cup watercress
   1 cup parsley
   1 tablespoon scallions
   1 clove garlic
   1 tablespoon salt
   1 cup Colombo Original Plain Yogurt

Wash watercress and parsley well. Remove heavy stems and measure loosely packed cups. Mince very fine or use a food processor. Add 2 tablespoons yogurt to facilitate fast chopping in processor. Add minced garlic and scallions; fold into yogurt and chill.

Onion Relish Dressing

Makes about 4 cups
   2 cups finely chopped Idaho-Oregon Sweet
      Spanish Onion (about 1 large)
   1 cup salad oil
   ½ cup catsup
   ½ cup vinegar
   ⅓ cup horseradish
   1 teaspoon salt
      Dash pepper
   ½ teaspoon dry mustard
      Juice of 1 lemon

Place chopped onion with remaining ingredients in a jar. Cover and shake until thoroughly blended. Refrigerate until used.

Avocado Dressing

Makes 1½ cups
   ⅓ cup milk
   1 cup creamed cottage cheese
   1 ripe avocado, peeled and cubed
   3 drops hot pepper sauce
      Dash onion powder

Put all ingredients into blender container. Cover and process at Blend until smooth.

Apricot-Honey Dressing

Makes 2 cups
   1 can (1 pound) apricots, drained
   ¼ lemon, seeded and peeled
   1 thin slice lemon rind, 1x2 inches
   ¼ cup honey
   ¼ teaspoon salt
   1 cup sour cream

Put apricots, lemon, and rind into blender; cover and process at Whip until apricots are puréed. Add honey, salt, and sour cream; cover and process only until well mixed.

Lime-Honey Fruit Dressing

Makes 1 cup
   1 piece lime peel, ½x1 inch
   ⅓ cup lime juice
   ⅓ cup honey
   ¼ teaspoon salt
   ¾ cup salad oil
   ½ teaspoon paprika
   ¾ teaspoon prepared mustard
   ½ teaspoon seasoned salt

Put all ingredients into blender. Cover and process at Grate until lime peel is grated.

Fruit Dressing

Makes ¾ cup
   ½ cup salad oil
   ¼ cup fresh lemon juice
   2 tablespoons honey
   1 teaspoon salt

Put all ingredients into blender. Cover and process at Whip until blended.

Index

To Order Other Volumes

If you would like to order extra volumes of the FAMOUS BRANDS COOKBOOK LIBRARY (if for any reason you have been unable to purchase any volume of the FAMOUS BRANDS COOKBOOK LIBRARY, or if you want additional copies for yourself or for giving as gifts), you may do so by sending a check or money order for the retail price plus $2.00 for postage and handling to:

Brand Name Publishing Corporation
1950 Craig Road
St. Louis, Missouri 63146
(Missouri residents add applicable sales tax)

Volume 1	**Desserts**	$1.99 plus $2.00 postage
Volume 2	**Every Oven Microwave Cookbook**	$3.99 plus $2.00 postage
Volume 3	**Great Vegetable Dishes**	$3.99 plus $2.00 postage
Volume 4	**Meat Cookbook**	$3.99 plus $2.00 postage
Volume 5	**Chicken & Poultry**	$3.99 plus $2.00 postage
Volume 6	**Breads, Quick Breads & Coffee Cakes**	$3.99 plus $2.00 postage
Volume 7	**Soups & Salads**	$3.99 plus $2.00 postage
Volume 8	**Pasta Dishes**	$3.99 plus $2.00 postage
Volume 9	**Fish & Seafood**	$3.99 plus $2.00 postage
Volume 10	**Cooking with Eggs & Cheese**	$3.99 plus $2.00 postage
Volume 11	**Main Dishes**	$3.99 plus $2.00 postage
Volume 12	**Chocolate Classics**	$3.99 plus $2.00 postage

FRENCH WHITE® COOKWARE
1½-Qt. Oval Casserole with Glass Cover

RETAIL VALUE: $23.00

THERMIQUE® THERMAL SERVER AND MUG SET

RETAIL VALUE: $46.00

VISIONS® RANGETOP COOKWARE
4-Piece Saucepan Set

RETAIL VALUE: $42.00

FRENCH WHITE® COOKWARE SET
2½-Quart Covered Round Casserole, 10" Pie Plate (Quiche), 2½-Quart Covered Oval Casserole, 1½-Quart Covered Round Casserole, 1½-Quart Open Oval Casserole, 1-Quart Oval Vegetable Dish, 8½" Pie Plate (Quiche), Two 15-Ounce Individual Oval Casseroles, and Two 16-Ounce Individual Round Casseroles

RETAIL VALUE: $155.90

SPECIAL OFFER
MADE ONLY TO BUYERS OF THE FAMOUS BRANDS COOKBOOK LIBRARY

BEAUTIFUL CORNING PRODUCTS

A Corning Ware® French White® 1½-Quart Oval Casserole with Glass Cover—retail value $23.00—yours FREE with 12 Proofs of Purchase (one from each volume) and $4.00 to cover postage and handling

and

By special arrangement, the COOKBOOK LIBRARY also offers incredible dollars off other selected Corning products, with total savings of up to $143.05.

Choose any—or all—of three Corning sets:

Visions® Rangetop 1½-Quart Covered Saucepan and 2½-Quart Covered Saucepan
Coupons available in Volumes 1 through 4
Retail Value $42.00
With 1 Coupon $29.95
With 2 Coupons $25.95
With 3 Coupons $21.95
postage and handling included

Thermique® 1-Liter Thermal Server with 4 Ceramic Mugs
Coupons available in Volumes 5 through 8
Retail Value $46.00
With 1 Coupon $31.95
With 2 Coupons $27.95
With 3 Coupons $23.95
postage and handling included

Corning Ware® French White® 14-Piece Cookware
Coupons available in Volumes 9 through 12
Retail Value $155.90
With 1 Coupon $ 74.95
With 2 Coupons $ 64.95
With 3 Coupons $ 54.95
postage and handling included

PLEASE TURN PAGE TO ORDER